Cooking with
Southern
Celebrities

COMPILED BY TRAVEL SOUTH USA

LONGSTREET PRESS
Atlanta, Georgia

Published by
LONGSTREET PRESS, INC.
2140 Newmarket Parkway
Suite 118
Marietta, Georgia 30067

Printed in the United States of America

1st printing 1992

Library of Congress Catalog Card Number 91-061942

ISBN 1-56352-014-X

This book was printed by Arcata Graphics Company, Kingsport,
Tennessee. The text was set in Adobe Times; cover page set in
Caslon 3.

Cover photo by Floyd Jillson.
Cover design by Jill Dible.

INTRODUCTION

The South is synonymous with good cooking. Whether it's Cajun-style seafood, flavorful country ham, spicy Creole, traditional cornbread, soul food or Low Country cooking, Southerners are proud of their cooking heritage and take every opportunity to share it with others. Even many festivals are food related; just another good reason for friends to get together and enjoy a variety of foods.

The South has also produced many outstanding individuals. Many Southerners — born or currently living in Alabama, Arkansas, Florida, Georgia, Kentucky, Louisiana, Mississippi, North Carolina, South Carolina, Tennessee and Virginia — have achieved greatness in the fields of music, drama, literature, art, sports, politics, science and business. Add to these notables the chefs from the numerous four- and five-star restaurants of the region, and you have an impressive group of dignitaries.

Combine the two specialties — celebrities and celebrated cuisine — and you've created "Cooking with Southern Celebrities." This cookbook offers a delectable collection of recipes from famous Southerners, and to give you insight into their personal lives, the celebrities included short travelogues of their favorite destination in the region.

This unique collection of delicious recipes from Southern celebrities has taken over two years to compile and produce. Unfortunately, during that time, a few well-loved and respected personalities have passed away. However, through their participation in this book, the fondness they had for their Southern roots as well as our cherished memories of those individuals will live on. So with the support of their families, we present their recipes for all to enjoy.

Most importantly, this book not only offers a tasty ingredient for selling the South, but it will also help feed the region's less fortunate. Partial proceeds from each book sold will be donated to food banks affiliated with Second Harvest, the nation's largest non-governmental food program. Second Harvest distributes food to more than 38,000 charitable agencies.

We hope you enjoy the cookbook. It embodies the best and most flavorful of the many culinary worlds represented in the South. But most of all, the real joy is sharing: sharing our Southern heritage and sharing our good fortune with foodbanks of the region.

Cooking with Southern Celebrities Staff

Editor
Kathryn Norton

Associate Editor
Tricia Sheldon

Concept and Research
Cheryl M. Hargrove

Recipe Collection
Meg Beasley

Recipe Testing
Chashe McNeil
Leslie Pittenger
University of Georgia
College of Home Economics

Design, Layout and Typesetting
Tricia Sheldon

Cover by
Longstreet Press

Divider Pages by
Janice Bauer-Manheim
Kennesaw State College
Art Department

Table of Contents

Appetizers 7

Soups & Salads
    Salads 17
    Soups 21

Breads 25

Entrees
    Beef 39
    Chicken 53
    Lamb and Game 70
    Seafood 74
    Eggs 87

Vegetables & Side Dishes 91

Desserts 109

Indexes
    Index by Recipe 137
    Index by Celebrity 142

Appetizers

Teddy Gentry

Born in Fort Payne, Alabama, Gentry is the bass guitarist for the country music group Alabama. The group's hit songs include "Why, Lady, Why," "Feels So Right," and "Mountain Music."

"The Gulf Coast of Florida would have to be one of my favorites. It's where I landed my first 105-pound tarpon."

Stuffed Bacon Rolls

12 slices bacon
1 medium onion, chopped
2 cloves garlic, minced
1 egg
$\frac{1}{2}$ cup tomato sauce
$\frac{3}{4}$ cup soft bread crumbs (1 slice)

1 can sliced mushrooms, drained (4 ounces)
2 tablespoons parsley, snipped
$\frac{1}{4}$ teaspoon salt
$\frac{1}{8}$ teaspoon pepper
1 pound ground beef

Partially cook bacon, set aside, reserving 2 tablespoons of drippings. Cook onion and garlic in reserved drippings till tender but not brown.

In bowl, combine egg and tomato sauce. Stir in all remaining ingredients except meat. Add meat, mix well. Divide the mixture into 4 parts.

Place 2 slices of bacon side-by-side on waxed paper. Cut another slice of bacon in half crosswise. Place the 2 half slices at one end of bacon slices, overlapping slightly.

Pat $\frac{1}{4}$ of mixture evenly over bacon. Roll up jelly-roll style, starting from narrow end. Place rolls seam side down on rack in 12 x $7\frac{1}{2}$ x 2-inch baking dish. Repeat with remaining bacon and meat and bake in 350° oven for about 40 minutes for medium doneness, or 1 hour for well done.

Makes 4 servings.

Bart Starr

Born in Montgomery, Alabama, Starr was the quarterback for the Green Bay Packers from 1956-71. He set several NFL passing records and was voted Most Valuable Player in the 1967 and 1968 Super Bowls, and was inducted into the Hall of Fame in 1977.

"My favorite destination today is Nashville, Tennessee. It is a beautiful city with its rolling hills, beautiful historic homes, warm, loving people and Civil War history. But I go there frequently because my favorite two little people live there, my granddaughters, Shannon and Jennifer Starr."

Cucumber Dip

1 block Philadelphia cream cheese (8-ounces)
½ cucumber (unpeeled)
¼ teaspoon dill weed
garlic salt to taste
2 heaping tablespoons Kraft mayonnaise

Finely grate cucumber, pour off and reserve juice. Blend all ingredients until creamy. If the dip is too thick, add reserved cucumber juice until right consistency.

Serving Suggestions:
Great dip with chips or crackers. Also makes nice spread for party sandwiches, open faced with thin cucumber slice on top or sprig of parsley.

Pimento Cheese Spread

1 package Kraft colby or medium aged Cheddar cheese (16 ounces), grated
1 jar chopped pimento (4 ounces)
½ cup sweet pickle relish
1 cup Kraft mayonnaise or enough to make to a spreading consistency

Mix all ingredients together.

Serving Suggestions:
This spread is excellent for sandwiches. We like toasted whole wheat bread, cheese spread and lettuce. Also good to serve to guests with crackers. Keeps very well. I keep it on hand all the time.

Ray Mabus

Born in Ackerman, Mississippi, Mabus is the governor of Mississippi.

"I like traveling all over the state of Mississippi, from the coast to the delta and to the rolling hills of north Mississippi. But what you have to understand is that I am a country boy and what I truly enjoy is going back to my hometown of Ackerman and visiting with family and friends."

Oysters Bienville

2 dozen oysters on the half shell
1/2 cup butter, softened (1 stick)
1/2 cup scallions, finely chopped
1/4 cup parsley, finely minced
1 1/2 teaspoons garlic, finely minced
1/2 cup flour
1/2 cup heavy cream
1 1/2 cups milk

4 egg yolks, beaten
1/4 cup dry sherry
1 teaspoon salt
1 teaspoon ground white pepper
1/2 teaspoon cayenne
2/3 cup finely diced mushrooms
1/2 pound boiled shrimp, diced

Melt the butter in a heavy saucepan. Add the scallions, parsley and garlic and simmer for about 8 minutes. Gradually add the flour and stir constantly for 2 to 3 minutes, until mixture is smooth. Add the milk and cream, stirring until mixture is creamy. Add the egg yolks, sherry, salt, pepper and cayenne. Mixture should begin to thicken. Add the mushrooms and stir for 1 minute. Add the shrimp and simmer for 3 to 4 minutes, until the sauce is quite thick. Remove to a shallow dish and refrigerate to chill.

Imbed shells in pans of rock salt. Bake at 350° for 10 minutes or until plump. Place under the broiler until brown.

Serve at once.

Vince Dooley

Born in Mobile, Alabama, Dooley is the athletic director and former head football coach at the University of Georgia.

"My favorite destination would have to be in my state of Georgia. I enjoy traveling to the mountains of north Georgia and to the seashores of south Georgia. As a matter of fact, I thoroughly enjoy traveling and can think of many places in all 11 Southern states that I would like to visit again."

Sweet Brie

1 round of brie not fully ripened, top rind
  removed (24 ounces)
1 cup chopped pecans or slivered almonds

2 cups brown sugar, firmly packed
crackers, wheat or stone

Preheat broiler. Place brie in a 10-inch quiche dish or pie plate and sprinkle with nuts. Cover top and sides with sugar, patting gently with fingertips. Do not worry if sides are not fully covered. Broil on lowest rack until sugar bubbles and melts, about 3 minutes.

Cheese should retain its shape. Watch carefully, it burns easily! Serve immediately.

Approximately 50 servings.

Jack Butler

Author of five published books including, Jujitsu for Christ *and* Nightshade, *Butler was born in Alligator, Mississippi, and now resides in Conway, Arkansas.*

"There's this island off the Gulf Coast of Florida, about five miles out in the bay. We like to rent a house in the off-season and live on the beach. I almost touched a dolphin in the water there once. You're crazy if you think I'm going to tell anybody where it is."

Tartare Good Old Boy

2 pounds lean round, chuck or sirloin
  ground coarsely, twice
2 teaspoons fresh-ground black pepper
1 teaspoon fresh-ground green pepper
1 teaspoon chili powder

1 teaspoon curry powder
3 cloves crushed garlic
½ teaspoon salt
1 tablespoon vinegar
salt to taste

Combine all ingredients, press into a mold and chill several hours. Turn out onto a serving platter. Serve with crusty bread or crackers. May be garnished with chopped hard-boiled eggs, capers or chopped onion.

Butler says, "I like to serve it with homemade hollandaise sauce, topped with caviar and dash each bit with hot sauce or pepper sauce."

Soups & Salads

Claude Pepper

Born in Dudleyville, Alabama, Pepper served as a Democratic senator from Florida, 1936 to 1951 and congressman from 1963 until his death in 1990. He was the oldest member of Congress and known as a spokesman for the aged.

Chunky Chicken Salad

1 medium chicken, cut up
poultry seasoning
salt and pepper to taste
1 pound white seedless grapes

6 ounces almonds, sliced
1 cup Hellmann's mayonnaise
spring onions
paprika

Add poultry seasoning generously to water in a large pot; bring to a boil. Add chicken and cook slowly until tender, about 1 hour. Remove chicken from bones and cut into medium-sized chunks. Add salt and pepper to taste and gently stir in grapes and almonds. Add mayonnaise and stir until well mixed. Chop spring onions and stir into chicken mixture to taste.

Serving Suggestions:
Place mound of chicken salad on bed of greens and sprinkle with paprika. Platter can be trimmed with additional grapes.

Serves 4.

Vanna White

Born in Conway, South Carolina, White is a model and TV personality. She became the hostess of the TV game show "Wheel of Fortune" in 1982.

Cottage Cheese Salad

1 small package Jell-O (I prefer lime)
1 pound small curd cottage cheese
1 can crushed pineapple, drained (16 ounces)
1 tub Cool Whip whipped topping (9 ounces)
pecans, optional

In large bowl, sprinkle Jell-O over cottage cheese. Fold in well. Drain the pineapple and fold into the cottage cheese. Fold in the Cool Whip and chill until ready to serve. You can also mix in pecans, but it's optional. Garnish with fruit.

Jim Varney

Born in Lexington, Kentucky, Varney is the actor and comedian who plays Ernest P. Worrell in several commercials and movies including Ernest Goes To Camp *and* Ernest Saves Christmas.

"Wherever you visit in Lexington, Kentucky, the hospitality shown you will make you want to return again and again. Southern people will not allow you to leave their homes without a token of their friendship, usually a gift of food."

Fresh Fruit with Orange-Pecan Dressing

2 cups mandarin oranges, drained
3 ripe bananas
4 kiwi fruit
2 cups sliced strawberries
1 fresh pineapple, sliced, or 1 can pineapple
    chunks
½ honeydew, diced
½ cantaloupe, diced

Sauce:
1 package cream cheese, softened (8 ounces)
2 tablespoons cream
⅓ cup undiluted frozen orange juice
1 teaspoon lemon juice
4 tablespoons sugar

Cut fruit into bite-sized pieces and place in 3-quart salad bowl. Mix sauce ingredients in small deep mixing bowl and beat on high speed until very creamy. Pour sauce over fruit into individual servings; do not pour over entire salad. Garnish with pecans as desired.

Serves 10-12.

Albert B. "Happy" Chandler

Born in Corydon, Kentucky, Chandler served as the Democratic governor of Kentucky, 1935-39 and 1955-59. He was baseball commissioner from 1945-51 and is a member of the Baseball Hall of Fame. He died in 1991.

"I'm a 'son of Pennyrile' and am very nostalgic about my section of western Kentucky, but since I made Woodford County my home in the early '20s, I have often said I don't like being out of the sound of the courthouse clock. There is no part of Kentucky I have not campaigned in, through, or visited during my two terms as governor, so I guess I have to opt out of choosing a favorite part. It's all beautiful and the people are the most welcoming in the United States."

Mary Alice's Salad Dressing

½ cup ketchup   ½ clove garlic
½ cup salad oil   ½ teaspoon salt
½ cup vinegar   pepper to taste

Pierce a garlic clove with toothpick or fork tines to release oil and place in pint jar with the other ingredients. Shake well just before pouring over salad greens.

May be prepared ahead; the salad dressing keeps well in air-tight container.

Serving Suggestions:
Makes a pretty salad poured into center of avocado half placed on bed of Kentucky Bibb lettuce.

Ellis Marsalis

Born in New Orleans, Louisiana, Marsalis is a jazz musician.

Crescent City Soup

1 package turtle soup mix ($\frac{1}{2}$ ounce)
1 tablespoon margarine
1 tablespoon flour
$\frac{1}{2}$ cup onions, chopped
4 toes garlic, chopped
1 cup prepared instant cream of chicken soup
1 tablespoon dill weed
1 teaspoon red pepper
1 tablespoon filé

$\frac{1}{2}$ pound shrimp, peeled and deveined
1 can smoked oysters (8 ounces)
1 can clams (8 ounces)
1 can tuna or salmon ($3\frac{1}{2}$ ounces)
salt and pepper to taste

Over medium heat in a 5-quart pot, prepare turtle soup according to package directions. Drain the canned seafoods, setting aside the liquid from both to be used later. While the soup is cooking, brown flour in margarine along with onions and garlic in a large skillet over medium heat, stirring constantly. Add chicken soup, the seafood liquids, dill weed and red pepper, one at a time while continuing to stir the mixture. Combine the filé with enough soup to make a smooth paste.

Bring mixture to a rapid boil and lower temperature to simmer for 5 minutes. Transfer to soup mixture, add seafood and continue to stir. Add salt and pepper to taste, lower heat to simmer and cook approximately 30 minutes.

Naomi Judd

Born in Ashland, Kentucky, Judd is the mother in the mother-daughter country duo The Judds, whose hits include "Love Can Build a Bridge," "Grandpa (Tell Me About the Good Old Days)," and "Mama, He's Crazy."

Hamburger - Vegetable Chowder

1 pound lean ground beef
3 tablespoons butter or oil
1 can of tomatoes with juice (14 ounces)
2 medium carrots, diced
½ cup diced celery

1 medium onion, chopped
2 teaspoons salt
¼ teaspoon pepper
1½ quarts water or V-8 juice
⅓ cup rice

Brown hamburger in oil over medium heat. Then add all other ingredients except the rice. Cook on low for 1 hour, then add rice. Cook until rice is done; add more water or tomato juice if it is too thick.

Makes 6 servings.

Jerry Lee Lewis

Born in Ferriday, Louisiana, Lewis is a singer and musician whose hits include "Great Balls of Fire" and "Whole Lotta Shakin' Goin' On."

"In February of 1985 I took my wife to Ferriday for the first time to see where I was born and raised. She loved it. In 1986 she drove back and got a ticket in Mississippi for speeding. I think she was in a hurry to get home!"

Perk Up Soup

2 large cans of Veg-All, large-cut vegetables
1 large can whole tomatoes
1 can baby English peas
4 beef bouillon cubes

$1\frac{1}{2}$ pounds ground chuck
1 tablespoon lemon pepper
touch of garlic

Cook ground chuck and set aside. Mix the remaining ingredients together and bring to boil. Add the ground chuck and simmer for 30 minutes.

Serve as appetizer or meal!

Breads

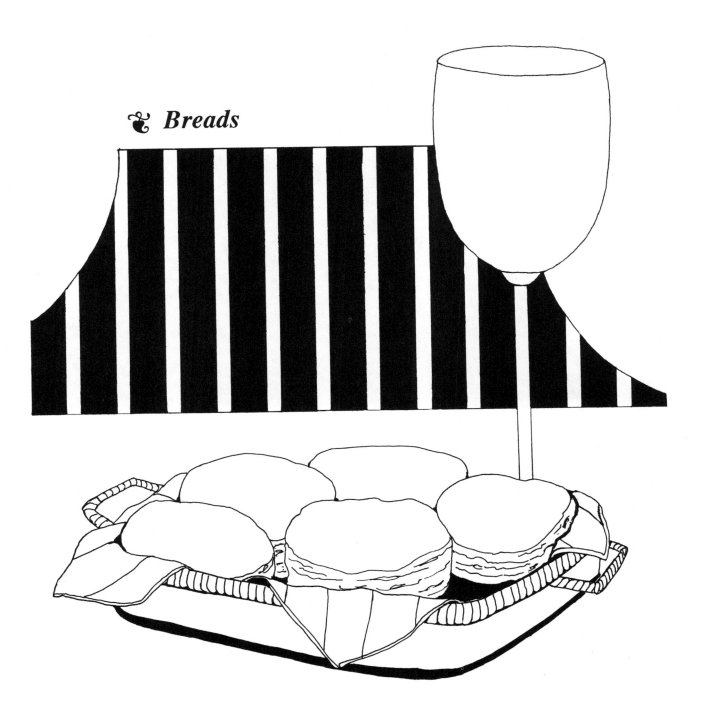

Wayne Newton

Born in Roanoke, Virginia, Newton is a singer and successful nightclub performer whose hit singles include "Danke Schoen" and "Daddy Don't You Walk So Fast."

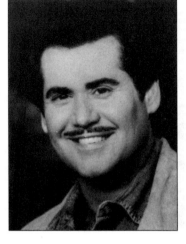

Bacon and Cheese Bread

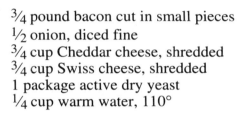

¾ pound bacon cut in small pieces
½ onion, diced fine
¾ cup Cheddar cheese, shredded
¾ cup Swiss cheese, shredded
1 package active dry yeast
¼ cup warm water, 110°

2 cups milk
2 tablespoons sugar
dash salt
3 tablespoons butter, melted
5 - 6 cups all-purpose flour

In a large bowl, dissolve yeast in warm water for 5 minutes. Add room temperature milk, butter, sugar and salt. Set aside. Saute bacon and onions until cooked well. Drain grease and cool.

Add about 4 to 4½ cups flour to the liquid until a sticky dough forms. Add bacon, onions and cheese, mixing well. Remove the dough from the bowl and place on a counter top or work area that has been dusted with flour. Knead the bread as you add more flour. Once the bread comes away from the kneading surface easily and becomes elastic, you have enough flour. Continue kneading for about 5 minutes. Roll into a ball and cut in half. Roll the halves into balls and place each one on a greased pan and cover with plastic film. Allow to rise for 2 to 3 hours.

Using your open palm, press down on risen dough to flatten. Roll dough into desired loaf shape and let rise for 1 hour. Place the loaves on an ungreased pan or sheet, brush with egg or milk and bake at 350° for 30 to 40 minutes. Remove and let cool at least a half hour before serving.

Makes 2 loaves.

Kenneth Noland

Born in Asheville, North Carolina, Noland is an artist whose paintings emphasize pure color and make color the subject.

"My favorite destination is Everglades City, Florida: snookfishing at dusk, when the tide and wind is right."

Lucy Ford's Cornbread

2 cups self-rising white corn meal or stone
   ground if available
pinch of salt
1 egg
1 cup buttermilk
1 tablespoon Crisco or rendered lard if available

Heat oven to 375° and kill a hog and render out the lard. Set aside cracklings if making cracklin' bread.

Mix dry ingredients and add buttermilk and a few drops of water if a moister bread is desired. Add the egg. Cook fat back, streaked bacon or Crisco in a black frying pan. Pour off about a tablespoon of grease into batter. Mix and add cracklins if desired. Keep skillet greasy and hot. Pour mix into skillet and put immediately into hot oven. When top of bread is a nice broken brown color, it's ready.

Lucy Ford's Biscuits

2 cups self-rising flour*
½ cup Crisco
½ cup buttermilk, more or less
½ or 1 level teaspoon salt

Mix dry ingredients thoroughly. Cut the lard into dry ingredients with a fork. Add the buttermilk and roll out the loosely mixed dough on a spread of flour and cut out large biscuits. The biscuits should be placed on baking sheet abutted (sides touching).
Bake at 425° until golden brown.

*If self-rising flour is not available, use flour with a pinch of baking soda and 2 level teaspoons of baking powder.

Beth Henley

Born in Jackson, Mississippi, Henley won the Pulitzer Prize in drama for her first full-length play, Crimes of the Heart. *She wrote the screenplay for the acclaimed film version which starred Diane Keaton, Jessica Lange, Sissy Spacek and Sam Shepard, and was nominated for an Academy Award.*

Spicy Hot Cornbread

1 can creamed corn
1 cup cornmeal
½ cup oil
1 cup buttermilk
½ teaspoon salt

1 large onion, chopped
2 hot peppers, chopped
2 eggs
6 ounces longhorn-style cheese, grated

Mix all of the ingredients together and bake in an 8 x 8-inch pan at 350° for 50 to 60 minutes. The cornbread will seem moist when done.

Tennessee Ernie Ford

Born in Bristol, Tennessee, Ford was a singer and a television star of the 1950s and '60s. He sang gospel and country music, including "Sixteen Tons," until his death in 1991.

"For me, a Southerner, it's next to impossible to choose one destination to be my favorite, so let me say this: Of course, going back to my home state of Tennessee has got to be my favorite. I never get tired of landing at Nashville or Tri-Cities up there near my hometown of Bristol in east Tennessee. When I land at either of these places or cross any border driving into Tennessee, I feel like I'm home.

"The beauty and lushness of Tennessee, any time of year, is always exciting to me. When I was a boy, I looked forward to fall and winter so we could hunt rabbits and squirrels. I still do and I'll never get tired of that. And Nashville, the way it's grown to be a great city, is gratifying, and the great Opryland complex is the eighth wonder of the world.

"If I could have a second favorite destination in the South it would have to be Arkansas. Nearly every year we go fishing out of Bull Shoals, Arkansas, on the White and the Buffalo rivers. What a thrill. Every fisherman in the country should take advantage of these beautiful rivers; it's one of the high points of my schedule every year.

"Then there's Louisiana. What a wonderful state, especially New Orleans. One of the great fun towns in our country. I've been there a hundred times and never tire of it. The food — a lot of it I'm sure is represented in this book — the entertainment, the music, the river — each one separately and all of them together make an exciting town in a great state.

"There is something wonderful in each of these 11 states I like, and I've been to all of them."

Pea-Picker's Cornbread

1 cup Martha White self-rising cornmeal
3 tablespoons Martha White self-rising flour
1 egg, beaten
2/3 cup buttermilk
1 tablespoon water
1 tablespoon melted shortening or bacon
　drippings

Preheat oven to 450°. Grease thoroughly and
heat (in the oven) a small black iron skillet, corn
stick or muffin pan.

Measure all ingredients in the order listed in a
mixing bowl and stir to blend thoroughly. Pour
batter into hot greased pan and bake 20 minutes
for sticks; 25 to 30 minutes for skillet or muffins.

Serve immediately with butter.

Note: There is no sugar in Pea-Picker's
cornbread. Only Yankees put sugar in
cornbread.

Old-Fashioned Cornbread Dressing

1 dozen cornbread muffins
skinless turkey neck
turkey heart
turkey gizzard
turkey liver
1 bay leaf
1/2 teaspoon dried onion
1/2 teaspoon parsley
1/8 teaspoon garlic salt
1/4 teaspoon salt
1/2 pound crumbled Jimmy Dean sausage
2 stalks celery, diced
1 medium onion, diced
1 1/2 teaspoons sage

Bake cornbread muffins according to directions
on package and set aside to cool.

In a medium sauce pan, place the turkey parts
with the bay leaf, dried onion, parsley, garlic salt
and salt. Cover with water and bring to a boil.
Simmer until the meat is tender, add water if
necessary to keep parts covered.

When cool, strip meat from neck and chop all
parts into real small pieces. Reserve broth.

In a skillet, saute the sausage, celery and onion.

Crumble the muffins. Add the sausage mixture,
chopped meat, sage, salt and pepper to taste.
Slowly add broth until the dressing is real moist.

Place in a 9 x 12-inch corning or baking dish and
bake uncovered for 25 to 30 minutes.

Jim Nabors

Born in Sylacauga, Alabama, Nabors is an actor and singer who played Gomer Pyle on "The Andy Griffith Show" and "Gomer Pyle, USMC."

"I have enjoyed traveling to and visiting all of the Southeastern states: Alabama, Arkansas, Florida, Georgia, Kentucky, Louisiana, Mississippi, North Carolina, South Carolina, Tennessee and Virginia. Each state is unique and special and offers everyone a wonderful experience with individual cultures, local cuisine and people.

"But Alabama, without a doubt, is my favorite as it is my home state. I have a special affinity for Alabama and its people. While it is moving towards economic growth and development, it still retains the Southern country charm and ethnicity I remember growing up. I moved away a long time ago, but a part of me is always there and I will forever carry a part of Alabama with me wherever I go."

Cornbread Dressing

4 cups cornbread, crumbled
2 cups bread crumbs
4½ cups chicken, pork or turkey stock, boiling

1 cup celery, chopped
½ cup onion, chopped
1 egg, beaten

Mix cornbread with bread crumbs and add boiling stock. Cover and set for 5 or 10 minutes. Add vegetables and mix well, then add egg and mix well. Bake in well-greased 9 x 13 x 2-inch pan at 375° for 45 minutes to 1 hour.

Makes 12 servings.

J. William Fulbright

Born in Sumner, Missouri, Fulbright served as a Democratic senator from Arkansas from 1945 to 1974. He wrote The Arrogance of Power *in 1966.*

Popovers

3 eggs, beaten
1 cup milk
1 cup flour
1 tablespoon butter, melted

Preheat oven to 450°. Beat egg, add milk, sifted flour and butter.

Place muffin tin, preferably cast iron, in hot oven for 10 minutes. Fill tin to $^2/_3$ full and bake for 15 minutes. Reduce heat to 350° and bake for another 10 minutes.

Do not open oven door during cooking.

Bob Timberlake

Born in North Carolina, Timberlake, an artist, has been honored by presidents Carter and Reagan at the White House and by Prince Charles at Buckingham Palace. He has served as the official artist of "Keep America Beautiful," and has had numerous sold-out, one-man exhibitions at New York's prestigious Hammer Galleries. His originals have been exhibited in many fine musuems, including the Corcoran Gallery in Washington, D.C., the North Carolina Museum of Art in Raleigh, the Isetan Gallery in Tokyo, Japan, and the Hubbard Musuem in Ruidoso Downs, New Mexico.

"Of the many places which I have been fortunate enough to visit in this great Southland of ours, I suppose none, as they say, can compare to my home. The warmth of family and friends close by is dear to me.

"There is one very special place, however, which I deeply enjoy, and that is my studio on Figure Eight Island just north of Wilmington, North Carolina. There is just something about the coast — about being near the sea. The power and majesty of the ocean and the timeless rolling of the waves — a reminder of how short and how precious our lives are."

Kay's Blueberry Muffins

1 cup plain flour
½ teaspoon salt
½ teaspoon soda
1 teaspoon baking powder
2 eggs

1 cup sour cream
5 tablespoons butter
1 cup brown sugar, firmly packed
1 cup old-fashioned oats
1 cup fresh blueberries, or frozen (do not defrost)

Preheat oven to 375° and grease muffin pans.

Set aside 2 tablespoons of flour to coat the blueberries. In a small bowl, combine the remaining flour, salt, baking powder and soda. In a large bowl, beat 2 eggs with sour cream until well blended. Melt the butter with the brown sugar and beat into the egg mixture. Stir in the oats. Fold in the flour mixture, stirring only enough to dampen the flour. The mixture should not be smooth. Toss the blueberries in the reserved flour and stir them into the batter. Spoon into the muffin pans, filling them ⅔ full. Bake for 25 to 30 minutes, until brown and puffy. Cool and remove from muffin tins.

Makes about 18 muffins.

Sam Nunn

Born in Perry, Georgia, Nunn has served as a conservative Democratic senator for Georgia since 1972 and the chairman of the Senate Armed Forces Committee since 1987.

"Georgia is special to me because it is home, but for any traveler, Georgia provides a wide variety of special experiences; from the blue-misted 'hills of Habersham' that inspired poet Sidney Lanier, to the coastal islands, with their moss-hung live oaks and many unspoiled beaches which were once the exclusive preserves of millionaires. Spring and fall are my favorite times to get away to a mountain cabin and spend time with my family in the woods as the seasons change. My daughter and I spent a unique vacation while she was home from college. We explored the Okefenokee Swamp, the remote, mysterious 'land of the trembling earth,' which is the source of both the Suwannee River and Walt Kelly's 'Pogo.'"

Georgia Peach Bread

3 cups sliced fresh peaches (5 large peaches)
2 cups all-purpose flour
$1/4$ teaspoon salt
1 teaspoon ground cinnamon
2 eggs

1 cup finely chopped pecans
1 teaspoon baking soda
$1^1/_2$ cups plus 6 tablespoons of sugar
$1/_2$ cup shortening
1 teaspoon vanilla

Place peaches and 6 tablespoons of sugar in blender and process until pureed. The mixture should yield about $2^1/_4$ cups. In mixing bowl, combine flour, baking soda, salt and cinnamon and set aside. In large bowl, cream sugar and shortening until mixed well. Add eggs and mix well. Alternately add dry ingredients with peach puree until all is mixed well. Stir in nuts and vanilla. Spoon batter into 2 well-greased and floured loaf pans. Bake at 325° for 55 to 60 minutes or until done. Cool 10 minutes in pan, turn on rack and cool completely.

Yields 2 loaves.

Entrees

Steve Lundquist

Born in Atlanta, Georgia, Lundquist won the Gold Medal in the 100-meter breaststroke during the 1984 Summer Olympics.

"Hilton Head Island, South Carolina, because it is so beautiful with the lighthouse and boats, and the recreational facilities like tennis, golf and swimming are wonderful. Hometown charm!"

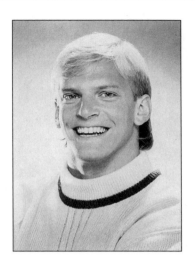

Anytime Brisket of Beef

3 to 4 pound brisket of beef
1 teaspoon salt
2 teaspoons celery seed
2 teaspoons Worcestershire sauce

2 tablespoons liquid smoke (Colgans)
1 teaspoon onion salt
1 teaspoon garlic salt
2 teaspoons pepper
1 cup barbeque sauce

Using your hands, cover all sides of beef with the salt, celery seed, Worcestershire sauce, liquid smoke, onion salt, garlic salt and pepper. Place the brisket in a large sheet of aluminum foil and wrap well around the meat. Set in baking pan and let stand in refrigerator overnight.

Bake in slow oven (300°) for 4 hours. Open foil and pour on barbeque sauce. Bake 1 additional hour in uncovered pan.

Serves 6.

William J. Guste, Jr.

Guste, whose family owns Antoine's Restaurant in New Orleans, is attorney general of Louisiana.

Guste Grits

2 cups grits
2 quarts water
3 teaspoons salt
6 ounces American cheese, grated, or you can
  substitute Swiss, Romano or sharp cheddar or
  a combination of all of them - WOW!

4 cloves garlic, pressed through garlic press
1 stick butter
3 eggs, slightly beaten
2 cups milk
grated Parmesan cheese, or a mixture of
  Parmesan, Romano, or best of all, Provolone

Cook the grits in the 2 quarts boiling salted water until tender but still pourable; in other words, don't let it thicken like a rock. Remove from heat and add the cheese, pressed garlic and butter. Let cool.

When cool, add in the eggs mixed with the 2 cups of milk. Pour the entire mixture into a 2-quart casserole that has been well greased with butter, margarine or salad oil. Bake at 325° for 50 minutes. Remove from oven and sprinkle the grated Parmesan or Romano cheese over the top and bake again for about 10 minutes more. Serve immediately.

As you can see, this can be prepared ahead of time. In this event, it should be kept refrigerated and baked until piping hot before serving.

Serving Suggestion:
It's great with grillades!

Grillades

4 pounds beef or veal round (½-inch thick)*
1 cup bacon drippings
½ cup flour
1 cup white onions, chopped
2 cups green onions, chopped
¾ cup celery, chopped
1 cup green peppers, chopped
4 cloves garlic, finely minced
2 cups tomatoes, chopped
1 can tomato sauce (8 ounces)

½ teaspoon tarragon vinegar, optional
1 sprig thyme, optional
1 cup water
1 cup red wine, or you can use water
3 teaspoons salt
½ teaspoon black pepper
2 bay leaves, optional
½ teaspoon of Tabasco
2 teaspoons of Worcestershire sauce
3 tablespoons of parsley, chopped

Remove the fat from the meat, cut into serving-size pieces and pound on wooden block to ½ inch thick. In dutch oven, brown the meat well in 4 tablespoons of bacon drippings. As the meat browns remove it from the dutch oven to a warm plate. Add 4 teaspoons of bacon drippings to the dutch oven and the half cup of flour. Stir and cook this until it turns a dark brown roux. Be careful once the roux starts to brown: it browns very rapidly, and if you don't watch it, it will burn. The color that you are trying to get in the roux is a color a little lighter than milk chocolate.

Add the onions, green onions, celery, peppers and the garlic to the roux and saute until they are limp. Add the tomatoes, tarragon and thyme. Cook for 3 or 4 minutes. Add the water and wine, stirring well for several minutes. Return meat to the dutch oven adding salt, pepper, bay leaves, Tabasco and Worcestershire sauce. Lower heat and continue cooking. Remove bay leaves, stir in parsley and let cool.

*If veal rounds are used, simmer covered for approximately 1 hour. If beef rounds are used, simmer covered approximately 2 hours.

Hopefully, you should let grillades sit several hours or overnight in the refrigerator before serving them. More liquid can be added to give your sauce the consistency you desire. But, by all means, be sure that the grillades are very tender.

Serve this over rice or the family version of Guste Grits.

Bert Lance

Born in Gainesville, Georgia, Lance is a banker and government official who served as the director of the Office of Management and Budget during the Carter administration in 1977.

Charcoaled Roast

3-pound rolled roast
salt
mustard
ice cream salt
charcoal

Salt and cover a 3-pound rolled roast with mustard. Roll in ice cream salt and refrigerate for 2 hours, until slight crust forms. Place over charcoal fire and turn as often as needed. Cook 1 hour for rare to $1\frac{1}{2}$ hours for medium done roast. Peel off crust and slice.

Walker Percy

Mark Morrow

Born in Birmingham, Alabama, Percy was a novelist whose books include The Moviegoer. *He died in 1990.*

"My favorite destination is Florida's Sanibel Island. A lovely island with good inns, reached by ferry from Fort Myers, and endless beaches with the greatest variety of shells I've ever seen. One walks, spots a jewel of a shell, picks it up, walks some more."

Salt Steak

Top-of-the-round beef, 2 inches thick
coarse "cattle" salt or ice cream salt
soy sauce

Pour a little water into half a bucket of coarse or "cattle" salt to make a slush. Mix well. Spread handfulls of salt mixture on both sides of steak, about $\frac{1}{4}$ inch thick. Cover with paper towels and clamp into a hand-held steak grill. Place the grill directly onto white hot briquets. Cook 12 minutes on each side, remove from heat, open and knock off salt with a hammer.

Serving Suggestion:
Slice thin and flavor with butter and soy sauce.

Burt Reynolds

Born in Waycross, Georgia, and living in Jupiter, Florida, Reynolds is an actor who has starred in numerous movies including Deliverance, *1972;* Smokey and the Bandit, *1977; and* The Best Little Whorehouse in Texas, *1982. He won the Emmy award in 1991 for best actor on CBS's "Evening Shade."*

"My favorite places in the South are both in Florida: my ranch in Jupiter, and Doak S. Campbell Stadium in Tallahassee, home of the Florida State Seminoles."

Burt's Beef Stew

3 slices of bacon, cut in small pieces
4 tablespoons flour
1 teaspoon salt
¼ teaspoon pepper
2 pounds lean beef (chuck is juicy) cut in 1-inch pieces
1 large onion, chopped (1 cup)
1 clove garlic, minced
1 can tomato sauce (15 ounces)

½ can condensed beef broth (5½ ounces)
1 cup good, dry Burgundy wine
1 bay leaf
1 pinch of thyme
2 carrots, cut up coarsely (1 cup)
2 stalks celery, cut up coarsely (¾ cup)
2 potatoes, pared and cut into pieces
6 to 8 mushrooms, sliced

Cook bacon until crisp in a large, heavy pot. Combine flour, salt and pepper. Dip beef in flour mixture to coat completely. Brown beef in bacon fat, turning often (add a little vegetable oil if needed). Add onion, garlic and brown slightly. Add tomato sauce, broth, wine, bay leaf and thyme. Cover and cook slowly for about 1 hour and 15 minutes. Add potatoes and cook for 15 minutes. Add carrots, celery and mushrooms and cook uncovered until meat and vegetables are tender.

Makes 4 servings.

Chris Evert

Born in Fort Lauderdale, Florida, Evert is a professional tennis player who held the number-one ranking, 1974-78 and 1980-81. She won three Wimbledons, seven French Opens, two Australian Opens, six U.S Open championships; a total of 18 Grand Slam titles which is the third best in the history of tennis. She was the first woman to reach $1 million in career tournament earnings.

"My favorite destination is the Polo Club of Boca Raton, Florida — it's home!"

John Russell

Chris's Spaghetti

6 pounds lean beef, minced
4 medium onions
7 tablespoons olive oil
5 cloves garlic, crushed
38 fluid ounces tomato juice

2 large cans tomato paste
1 large can mushroom stems and pieces
2 tablespoons oregano
2 bay leaves, halved
1 tablespoon salt

Brown the beef, onions and garlic in olive oil. Add remaining ingredients and simmer for 1 hour, stirring occasionally. Serve over freshly cooked spaghetti. Leftovers can be frozen.

Serves 12.

George Hamilton, IV

Born in Winston-Salem, North Carolina, Hamilton is a country music entertainer.

"Grandfather Mountain, North Carolina, because of fond memories of many family visits to 'the singin' on the mountain' festival in June and the Highland Games in July. Our entire family has shared the enjoyment of the natural beauty of 'Grandfather' during all seasons of the year and the wildlife habitat where we can all see and enjoy bear, deer and cougar in a natural setting."

Corned Beef Casserole

1 can corned beef or corned beef hash	1 medium onion, minced
1 small box elbow noodles, cooked and drained	1 can cream of chicken soup
1 cup cheese, grated	buttered bread crumbs

Mix noodles, corned beef, cheese and onions in baking dish. Put undiluted soup on top and add bread crumbs. Cook in 325° oven for about 30 to 40 minutes. Don't burn bread crumbs. Cover if it gets too hot.

To make bread crumbs:
Bake 4 slices of bread in oven until hard. Grate and mix with a stick of melted butter.

Stan Smith

*Born in Pasadena, California, and residing on Hilton
Head Island, South Carolina, Smith is a professional
tennis player who holds 26 U.S. singles and doubles titles,
including the U.S. Open singles, 1971, and U.S. Open
doubles, 1968, 1974, 1978 and 1980. Smith also won
Wimbledon in 1972.*

*"Hilton Head, South Carolina. It's home for my family
and me. We all spend time on the tennis courts at Sea
Pines Plantation. We have traveled all over the world and
this is our favorite spot!"*

Michael Baz

Sloppy Joe's

2 pounds ground beef
2 cans bean and bacon soup (11½ ounces)
1 cup catsup
1 teaspoon chili powder

4 tablespoons sugar
½ cup water
4 tablespoons barbecue sauce

Brown ground beef and drain fat. Add the remaining ingredients and heat thoroughly.
Serve over open hamburger buns.

Richard Petty

Born in Level Cross, North Carolina, Petty is an auto racer who has won more grand national stock car races than any other driver. He announced his retirement in 1991.

"Our race team travels several thousand miles during the year to approximately 12 different states. I guess my favorite destination is always the trip back home."

Stuffed Bell Peppers

1½ pounds ground beef
1 medium onion, chopped fine
1 tablespoon chili powder
2 eggs
1 cup catsup
1 cup corn flakes
salt and pepper to taste
6 green, red or yellow bell peppers, cut in half
　　and cleaned

Sauce:
2½ cups catsup and tomato paste, use more
　　catsup than paste
2 tablespoons brown sugar
2 tablespoons ground mustard
1 tablespoon vinegar

Boil peppers for 5 minutes. Mix other filling ingredients together. Stuff peppers with mixture and arrange in bottom of large pyrex dish. Mix sauce ingredients together and pour over peppers. Bake at 375° for 30 to 40 minutes.

Ned Beatty

Born in Louisville, Kentucky, Beatty is an actor who has appeared in films including Deliverance, *1972, and* Superman, *1978.*

"My favorite destination is Appalachia. Within this area, crossing most states included in this cookbook, my first choice is Whitesburg, a small Kentucky mountain town. It is the home of Appalshop, a media cooperative that through the use of radio, television, film, recording and print media tells the story of Appalachian culture and concerns. And the Courthouse Cafe has good pie. P.S. Holding an actor to 50 words is a lot like picking your hound up by the ears ... it may be fun for you ...."

Hungarian Goulash

1 tablespoon oil
1 green pepper, chopped
1 onion, chopped
1 clove garlic, chopped
1½ pounds ground beef
1 large can tomatoes

1 small can tomato sauce
2 teaspoons sugar
salt and pepper to taste
¾ pound cooked spaghetti
½ pound cheddar cheese, grated

Saute the green pepper, onion and garlic in small amount of oil. Add meat and cook until done. Add tomatoes, tomato sauce, sugar, salt and pepper, simmer for 30 minutes. Add cooked spaghetti and mix well. Place in casserole and top with grated cheese. Bake in 350° oven for 30 minutes or until bubbly hot.

Beatty says: "This recipe is just a cheap good meal. I think it's kind of fun that we called it Hungarian Goulash! Sounds important, though."

Harry Langdon Photography

Rosemary Clooney

Born in Maysville, Kentucky, Clooney is a singer who had the million-selling single "Come On-a My House" in 1951 and wrote the autobiography This for Remembrance *in 1979.*

"My favorite Southern destination would have to be my home state of Kentucky. I have a home in Augusta and always look forward to the time I can spend there."

Viennese Goulash

¾ cup butter
2 teaspoons tomato paste
2 teaspoons marjoram, crushed
1 teaspoon caraway seeds, crushed
1 teaspoon lemon rind, finely chopped
1 clove garlic, crushed

1½ pounds onions, sliced
1½ tablespoons paprika
2 pounds beef chuck, rump or round, cut into chunks
1 cup water
salt to taste

In large saucepan combine the butter, tomato paste, marjoram, caraway seeds, lemon peel and garlic. Add onions and saute, stirring constantly, until they are golden. Add paprika and cook for about 1 minute, stirring constantly. Add beef, water and salt to taste. Cover the saucepan tightly and simmer until the beef is tender, about 2 hours. If necessary, add more water while cooking. Just before serving, add ½ cup water and let the sauce boil up once.

Serving Suggestion:
Serve the goulash with noodles or boiled potatoes.

Ray Stevens

Born in Clarkdale, Georgia, Stevens is a country music singer and comedian with such hit songs as "The Streak," "Shriner's Convention," and "Misty."

Slick Lawson

Raymone's Beanie Weenies

1 medium onion, diced
1 green bell pepper, diced
2 celery sticks, chopped
½ pound ground beef

1 package wieners
1 large can baked beans
1 cup brown sugar
Tabasco sauce

Saute the onion, green pepper and celery in butter until the onions look slightly opaque. Transfer this mixture to a large pot and set aside. Crumble and brown ground beef, drain grease and transfer meat to pot with onion mixture. Drain baked beans, remove any pork fat and add to large pot. Cut wieners into bite-size pieces and add to pot. Stir in brown sugar and add Tabasco sauce to taste. Heat thoroughly over low temperature and serve.

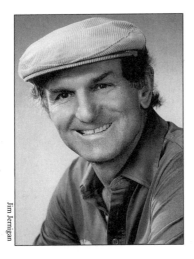

Jim Jernigan

Don Garlits

Garlits is a drag racer known as the "King of Speed." A native of Florida, he was the first man to crack the 200 mph barrier, in 1964, and the first to hit 250 mph for the quarter mile, in 1975.

Horkies
(pigs in a blanket)

1 large head cabbage
2 pounds stew beef, ground with 1½ pounds
  pork
½ cup rice
1 egg

1 medium size onion, chopped
1 teaspoon salt
dash pepper
1 can tomatoes (16 ounces)
1 can tomato sauce (8 ounces)

Wash and parboil head of cabbage in salted water for about 5 minutes, turning once. Remove from water and drain on paper towels, saving water.

Mix meat, onion, rice, salt, pepper and beaten egg in a bowl. Roll meat into oblong balls and wrap in single cabbage leaf. Place in bottom of large pot. When all of the meat has been wrapped, chop up remaining cabbage and cover top of meat mixture. Cover with tomatoes, tomato sauce and reserved liquid. Simmer slowly for 2 hours, covered.

Elizabeth Dole

Born in Salisbury, North Carolina, Dole began her tenure as president of the American Red Cross, the nation's preeminent human and social services organization, in February 1991. Prior to coming to the Red Cross, she served six United States presidents in a career which has seen her named by the Gallup Poll as one of the world's 10 Most-Admired Women. She served as secretary of labor during the Bush administration from 1987 to 1991 and was the nation's longest-serving secretary of transportation during the Reagan administration from 1983 to 1987. Prior to becomming secretary of transportation, Dole served as assistant to President Reagan for public liaison from 1981 to 1983, as a federal trade commissioner from 1973 to 1979 and as deputy director of the White House Office of Consumer Affairs from 1971 to 1973.

"I would have to say that one of my favorite destinations is Salisbury, North Carolina. It is my home and where my mother still lives."

Chicken and Wild Rice Casserole

1 package of long grain and wild rice (6 ounces)
½ cup chopped onion
½ cup margarine
¼ cup flour
1 can mushrooms (6 ounces)
chicken broth

3 cups cooked chopped chicken
¾ teaspoon salt
¼ cup cream or milk
1 jar chopped pimento (4 ounces)
½ cup slivered almonds

Prepare rice according to directions on box. Cook onion in margarine and stir in flour. Drain mushrooms, reserving liquid. Add chicken broth to mushroom liquid to make 1½ cups and stir liquids into flour mixture. Add cream and cook until thick. Add remaining ingredients except almonds.

Place in a 2- to 4-quart casserole and sprinkle with almonds. Bake at 350° for 20 to 30 minutes.

Freezes well.

Don Tyson

Born in Springdale, Arkansas, Tyson is the chairman of Tyson Foods.

"Cape Carteret, North Carolina, and Key West, Florida, for the great fishing!"

Roast Boneless Chicken Legs with Apricot-Pecan Stuffing

20 chicken legs, boneless
32 ounces apricot nectar
16 ounces orange juice, strained
8 ounces cider vinegar

1 tablespoon lemon juice
1 teaspoon mustard powder
1 teaspoon ginger, ground

Place frozen legs in full-sized steam table pan. Do not stack more than one layer. Combine apricot nectar, orange juice, cider vinegar, lemon juice, mustard powder and ground ginger in bowl. Mix well. Pour over frozen legs and marinate for 4 hours. Strain off marinade and dry chicken. Spread 3 ounces of stuffing on each portion, roll and tie in 3 places. Place tied legs on sheet pan, roast at 350° until done, about 45 minutes to 1 hour.

Apricot-Pecan Stuffing

8 ounces apricots, dried
2 ounces brandy
16 ounces water, hot
1 pound butter, melted
8 ounces onions, minced
1 pound pork sausage, crumbled
1 pound cornbread crumbs, fresh

6 ounces pecans, chopped
2 ounces parsley, chopped
1 teaspoon thyme, dried
½ teaspoon sage, ground
1 teaspoon white pepper
salt to taste
apricot liquid, as needed

Combine dried apricots, brandy and hot water in small bowl. Let soak for 30 minutes. Drain well, reserving liquid. Chop and reserve apricots. Saute onions in butter until golden, strain and reserve onions and butter. Return the butter to pan. Saute sausage in hot butter until browned, then transfer to a large bowl. Add the reserved onions and apricots. Add cornbread crumbs, pecans, parsley, thyme, sage, salt and white pepper to the apricot mixture and mix well. Add reserved apricot liquid to adjust consistency as desired.

Apricot Mustard Sauce

64 ounces apricot preserves
6 ounces Dijon-style mustard
1 ounce honey
1 ounce brandy

Simmer preserves over gentle heat to melt. Add mustard, honey and brandy to the preserves. Heat to simmer, and simmer 5 minutes. Spoon over boneless legs.

Ronnie Milsap

Born in Robbinsville, North Carolina, Milsap is a country music performer whose hit songs have included "Almost Like A Song," "Smoky Mountain Rain" and "Any Day Now."

"My favorite destination, naturally, is North Carolina. That's where I was born and raised, and just getting the opportunity to visit my home area at the fork of the Smokies always gives me an inner peace and perspective I don't seem to get anywhere else in the world. I made the statement in my autobiography that 'memories never die in the mountains,' and that's right ... they don't!"

Chicken Breast Casserole

6 chicken breasts, cooked, skinned and boned
2 packages frozen broccoli, cooked
2 cans cream of chicken soup
1 cup mayonnaise

1 teaspoon lemon juice
1 cup medium cheddar cheese, shredded
bread crumbs

In casserole dish, mix together broccoli, soup, mayonnaise and lemon juice. Place chicken breast on top of mixture. Top with cheese and bread crumbs and bake at 350° for 30 minutes.

Bill Clinton

Born in Hope, Arkansas, Clinton is the Democratic governor of Arkansas and a presidential candidate in 1992.

"A favorite destination in Arkansas is a trip to Mountain View to visit the Ozark Folk Center State Park and Blanchard Springs Caverns. The Folk Center is an interpretive cultural center which preserves the arts, crafts, music and lore of Ozark Mountain people. A guided tour of nearby Blanchard Caverns complements the visit."

Chicken Enchiladas

cooking oil
2 cans green chilies (4 ounces), seeded and chopped
1 large clove garlic, minced
1 can tomatoes (28 ounces)
2 cups onion, chopped
2 teaspoons salt

½ teaspoon oregano
3 cups cooked chicken, shredded
2 cups dairy sour cream
2½ cups cheddar cheese, grated
1 teaspoon salt
15 corn tortillas

Preheat oil in skillet, add chilies and minced garlic and saute.

Drain and break up tomatoes, reserving ½ cup liquid. Add tomatoes, onion, teaspoon salt, oregano and reserved tomato liquid to chili mixture. Simmer uncovered until thick, about 30 minutes. Remove from skillet and set aside.

Combine chicken with sour cream, 2 cups grated cheese and 1 teaspoon salt. Heat ⅓ cup oil. Dip tortillas in oil until they become limp, drain well on paper towels. Fill tortillas with chicken mixture. Roll up and arrange side by side, seam down, in 9 x 13 x 2-inch baking dish. Pour chili sauce over enchiladas and top with remaining grated cheese. Bake at 250° until heated through, about 20 minutes.

Recipe taken from *Thirty Years at the Mansion* by Elizabeth Ashley.

Terry Bradshaw

Born in Shreveport, Louisiana, Bradshaw was quarterback for the Pittsburgh Steelers from 1970 to 1984, and voted Most Valuable Player for Super Bowls XIII and XIV.

"I grew up in Shreveport, Louisiana, and I think it is a good place to raise children. However, since marrying my wife Charla, we have two children, Rachel and Erin, and we live in Southlake, Texas. Since I travel so much, I probably will never get to see all of it, but I love the South. I would never live anywhere else."

Chicken Melanzana with Spaghetti

2 whole large chicken breasts
garlic salt
freshly ground pepper
½ teaspoon Italian seasoning
½ cup chopped onion

1 can tomato paste (6 ounces)
1 small eggplant, peeled and sliced
1 cup water
3 cups tender cooked spaghetti

Season the chicken pieces and place the skin side up in a shallow roasting pan. Quick bake in a 450° oven for 15 to 20 minutes, until well browned. Pour off all fat. Combine the other ingredients except for the spaghetti and surround the chicken. Cover the roaster loosely with foil and bake at 350° for 40 to 50 minutes, stirring occasionally until the chicken is tender and the liquid has reduced for a thick sauce.

Serve with ¾ cup tender cooked spaghetti per person. Makes 4 servings, 297 calories each. This recipe represents all food groups; serve with a salad.

DaveyAllison

Born in Hollywood, Florida, and raised in Alabama,
Allison is a Winston Cup race car driver.

"As a young boy growing up in Alabama, I found myself
around fishing and hunting camps in central Alabama.
Dad and Uncle Donnie have always been avid hunters and
fishermen. I enjoy sights and attractions everywhere I go,
but Alabama has to be the most beautiful."

Chicken Spectacular

1 jar dried beef
6 boneless chicken breasts
6 slices bacon
1 cup sour cream
1 can cream of mushroom soup

Layer bottom of 9 x 12-inch casserole dish with dried beef. Roll each chicken breast up and wrap
with slice of bacon. Use toothpick to hold together. Lay breasts on top of dried beef. Mix together
in a separate bowl, 1 cup of sour cream and a can of mushroom soup. Pour over chicken and cover
with foil. Bake at 275° for 3 hours. Take foil off last 10 minutes to brown.

Gene Maggio, NY Times Studio

Craig Claiborne

Born in Sunflower, Mississippi, Claiborne is the food editor for the New York Times *and the author of* The New New York Times Cookbook.

"I have, for the past several years, spent most of my birthdays at a small inn in Washington, Virginia. It is known quite simply as The Inn at Little Washington, to disassociate its location from Washington, D.C. which is two hours away.

"I first went there on hearsay from friends who extolled the virtues of its food and interior. At the time of my visit it had fewer than a dozen guest rooms and the food was, in all respects, superior. It has an international menu but I was impressed to find one Southern specialty of my childhood on the menu — black-eyed peas. Not just ordinary black-eyed peas cooked for hours with ham hock, but black-eyed peas vinegarette. The peas were served cold with an exceptional salad dressing made with finely chopped garlic, parsley, balsamic vinegar and a fine olive oil. I wrote about the experience with exuberance and it appeared in the New York Times.

"For my birthday the following September, I returned to the inn with a friend, and scattered about the rooms were copies of my recently published autobiography titled A Feast Made for Laughter. *In my bedroom was a copy of* Fevers, Floods and Faith, A History of Sunflower County, Mississippi, 1844-1976, *a book in which my family was prominently mentioned.*

"I had mentioned in my autobiography that I had first sampled and fell in love with foreign food (I was raised on soul food) during the invasion of North Africa while serving in the U.S. Navy during World War II. When I went to dinner that evening, one small room had been cordoned off and the table was furnished with reproductions of traditional Moroccan platter, urns and all the rest, and I was served an authentic Moroccan meal.

"In my travels South, I almost invariably travel by air to Memphis, Tennessee, before driving to my family's residence in the Mississippi delta. I arrive in Memphis around noon and stop at Gridley's Barbecue House on Elvis Presley Drive. I feast to my heart's content on Gridley's excellent barbecue, some of the best in the South."

My Mother's Chicken Spaghetti

1 chicken with giblets (3½ pounds)
chicken broth
salt
3 cups canned Italian tomatoes, peeled
7 tablespoons butter, divided
3 tablespoons flour

½ cup whipping cream
⅛ teaspoon grated nutmeg
freshly ground pepper to taste
⅓ pound fresh mushrooms
2 cups onion, finely chopped
1½ cups celery, finely chopped

1½ cups green pepper, chopped
1 tablespoon or more garlic, finely minced
¼ pound ground beef
¼ pound ground pork
1 bay leaf

½ teaspoon hot red pepper flakes, optional
1 pound spaghetti or spaghettini
½ pound Cheddar cheese, grated (2 to 2½ cups)
grated Parmesan cheese

Note: Ingredients must be prepared at least 4 hours before baking.

Place the chicken with neck, gizzard, heart and liver in a kettle, add chicken broth to cover and salt to taste. Bring to boil and simmer until chicken is tender without being dry, 35 to 45 minutes. Cool and remove the chicken and take the meat from the bones. Shred the meat, cover and set aside.

Return the skin and bones to the kettle and cook the stock 30 minutes or longer. Strain and reserve the broth. There should be 4 to 6 cups of broth.

Place tomatoes in a saucepan and cook down to half the original volume, stirring. There should be 1½ cups. Melt 3 tablespoons butter in a saucepan and add flour, stirring to blend with a wire whisk. When smooth, add 1 cup of reserved hot broth and the cream, stirring rapidly with the whisk. When thickened and smooth, add the nutmeg, salt and pepper. Continue cooking, stirring occasionally, about 10 minutes. Set aside.

Heat 1 tablespoon butter in a small skillet and add the mushrooms. Cook, shaking the skillet occasionally, stirring until golden brown. Heat 3 tablespoons butter in a deep skillet and add the onions. Cook, stirring until wilted. Add the celery and green pepper and cook, stirring, about 5 minutes. Do not overcook. The vegetables should be crisp-tender. Add the garlic, beef and pork and cook, stirring and chopping down with the edge of a metal spoon to beak up meat. Cook just until the meat loses its red color. Add the bay leaf, red pepper flakes, tomatoes, white sauce and mushrooms.

Cook the spaghetti in boiling salted water until it is just tender. Do not overcook. It will cook again when blended with the chicken and meat sauce. Drain the spaghetti and run under cold water.

Spoon enough of the meat sauce over the bottom of a 5- or 6-quart casserole to cover it lightly. Layer ⅓ of the spaghetti, ⅓ of the shredded chicken, a layer of meat sauce and a layer of grated Cheddar cheese. Continue making layers, ending with a layer of spaghetti topped with a thin layer of meat sauce and cheese. Pour in up to 2 cups of the reserved chicken broth or enough to almost but not quite cover the top layer of spaghetti. Cover and let spaghetti stand for 4 to 6 hours.

If the liquid is absorbed as the dish stands, add a little more chicken broth. When ready to bake, preheat the oven to 350°. Place the spaghetti casserole on top of the stove and bring it just to boil. Cover and place it in the oven. Bake 15 minutes and uncover. Bake 15 minutes longer or until the casserole is hot and bubbling throughout and starting to brown on top.

Serving Suggestion:
Serve immediately with grated Parmesan cheese on the side. When this dish is baked and served, the sauce will be just a bit soupy rather than thick and clinging.

Serves 12 or more.

From Craig Claiborne's *Favorites from the New York Times,* Volume II.

Brooks Robinson

Born in Little Rock, Arkansas, Robinson played third base for the Baltimore Orioles from 1955 to 1977. Known for fielding, he was voted the American League's Most Valuable Player in 1964 and inducted into the Baseball Hall of Fame in 1983.

"My favorite destination in Arkansas is Little Rock. I not only grew up there, but can't wait to get back to my mother's home cooking ... fried okra, cornbread and chicken."

Chicken, Broccoli and Rice Casserole

1 medium onion, chopped
3 tablespoons margarine
1 can cream of chicken soup
½ cup milk
½ pound Velveeta cheese, additional needed for
   topping

3 cups cooked rice, not instant
2 packages frozen chopped broccoli, thawed
2 cups boneless chicken breast, cooked and
   chopped
chopped almonds, optional

Saute onion in margarine. In a double boiler, combine onion, cream of chicken soup, milk and ½ pound of Velveeta cheese. Heat until cheese melts. Fold in rice, broccoli and chicken. Pour into greased shallow casserole dish. Put strips of Velveeta and almonds on top (optional) and bake at 350° for 30 minutes.

Can be prepared early and refrigerated to bake later.

Al Gore, Jr.

Born in Tennessee, Gore is a moderate Democratic U.S. senator from Tennessee who ran for president in 1988.

Chinese Chicken with Walnuts

1 1/2 pounds whole chicken breasts, skinned, boned and split and cut into 1-inch pieces
3 tablespoons soy sauce
2 teaspoons cornstarch
2 tablespoons dry sherry
1 teaspoon sugar
1 teaspoon fresh ginger root, grated

1/2 crushed red pepper
2 tablespoons cooking oil
2 medium green peppers, cut into 3/4-inch pieces
4 green onions, bias-sliced into 1-inch lengths
1/2 cup walnut halves
1/2 teaspoon salt

Blend soy sauce into cornstarch, stir in sherry, sugar, ginger root, red pepper and salt.

Preheat wok or large skillet over high heat. Add cooking oil. Stir-fry green peppers and onions in hot oil for 2 minutes. Remove. Add walnuts to wok. Stir-fry 1 to 2 minutes or until golden. Remove. Add more oil if necessary.

Add 1/2 chicken. Stir-fry for 2 minutes. Remove. Stir-fry remaining chicken for 2 minutes. Return chicken to wok. Stir soy mixture and add to chicken. Cook and stir until bubbly. Stir in vegetables and walnuts, cover and cook for 1 minute.

Serves 6.

Chef Paul Prudhomme

Born in Opelousas, Louisiana, Prudhomme is the chef and owner of K-Paul's Restaurant in New Orleans.

"Whenever the fast pace of the city gets me down, I hop in my truck and head for Acadiana — the Cajun country of south Louisiana, where I was born. Life in Acadiana has a gracious and relaxed pace, set by the rhythms of the seasons and tides. People take time to linger over a cup of chicory coffee and chat, en francais, with old friends. Go down to the landing and watch the old boats come in, loaded down with the freshest shrimp you can imagine. Or spend a day in the farm country, stopping by the roadside to buy homemade boudin and cracklings. Wherever you go in south Louisiana, you will find marvelous food, and even more marvelous people. So when it's time to leave and everyone says 'Come back and see us soon' ... you can bet that I will!"

Corn and Chicken Casserole

3 tablespoons Chef Paul Prudhomme's Poultry Magic®
2 chickens (2 to 3 pounds each), cut into 10 pieces
1/3 cup vegetable oil
2 quarts fresh corn, cut off the cob (about 12, 8-inch ears)

3 1/2 cups finely chopped onion
1 1/2 cups finely chopped green bell peppers
1 pound peeled, chopped tomatoes
3 1/2 cups chicken stock
2 cups raw rice, preferably converted

Remove excess fat from the chickens and cut each into 10 pieces. Season the chicken pieces with 2 tablespoons of the seasoning and place in a sealable plastic bag in the refrigerator overnight.

Take the chicken out of the refrigerator and let set at room temperature. Heat the oil in an 8-quart roasting pan over high heat until it just starts to smoke, about 6 minutes. Add the 10 largest pieces of chicken and brown, skin side down first, cooking 5 minutes on each side. Remove the chicken and reheat the oil about 1 minute or until the oil stops sizzling. Brown the remaining chicken for 5 minutes on each side. Remove and keep warm.

Add half of the corn (1 quart) to the hot oil. Scrape the bottom of the pan well to get up all the browned chicken bits and stir to mix well. Let the corn cook, without stirring, for about 6 minutes. You want it to brown and the starch to start breaking down. Add half of the remaining seasoning and stir to incorporate. Let the mixture cook, without stirring, about 7 minutes to continue the browning process.

Stir in the onions, bell peppers, and the last of the seasoning. Cover with a tight-fitting lid and cook for about 5 minutes.

Add the remaining corn and the tomatoes. Stir to mix well and re-cover. Cook for 10 minutes.

Transfer the corn mixture to another pan and keep warm. Preheat oven to 400°F.

Add the stock and the rice to the roasting pan. Bring to a boil, stirring occasionally. Layer the chicken pieces on top of the rice and cover the chicken layer with the corn mixture. Put the lid back on and bake in a 400° oven for 25 minutes.

Remove the casserole from the oven, but don't take the lid off. Let it sit for 10 minutes covered and then serve.

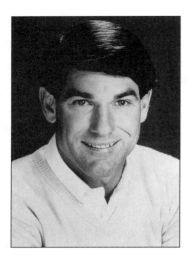

Steve Garvey

Born in Tampa, Florida, Garvey played first base for the Los Angeles Dodgers from 1969 to 1982 and the San Diego Padres from 1983 to 1987. He holds many major league fielding records and is a 10-time National League All-Star.

"My favorite destination is Tampa, Florida. I enjoy trips to Tampa as it is my former home and, as such, holds many memories for me. In addition, I see Tampa as a city which features 'all-American living' — a city that is progressive. To me, Tampa is the 'heart of Florida.'"

Hawaiian Barbecue Chicken

4 to 6 chicken breasts
1 pint barbecue sauce
1 can crushed pineapple

Mix barbecue sauce and pineapple, pour over chicken and bake at 400° for 1 hour.

Serving Suggestion:
Serve with yellow rice, mixed vegetables, etc.

Tommy Newsom

Born in Portsmouth, Virginia, Newsom is the assistant music director of "The Tonight Show Starring Johnny Carson," until 1992.

"My favorite place is Williamsburg, Virginia. It is 60 miles from where I grew up and it continues to fascinate me. The whole area is loaded with history and the country is beautiful. Jamestown, Yorktown and Williamsburg itself can take you from the first settlement of the country through the Revolutionary and Civil wars."

Lemon Chicken Scallopini

2 large chicken breasts, split, skinned and boned
¾ teaspoon salt
½ teaspoon freshly ground pepper
4 teaspoons cornstarch
4 teaspoons vegetable oil
1 egg white

flour
4 tablespoons butter or margarine
1 lemon, very thinly sliced
2 tablespoons fresh lemon juice
1 large clove garlic, minced
2 tablespoons minced parsley

Place each piece of chicken breast between 2 sheets of waxed paper and pound with meat pounder or cleaver until flat, about ¼ inch thick. Place the chicken in glass pie plate and sprinkle with ¾ teaspoon salt and ½ teaspoon freshly ground pepper and let stand 20 minutes.

Sprinkle the chicken with cornstarch and oil, gently turn to mix, and let stand 20 minutes. Fold in unbeaten egg white and let stand 30 minutes. Shake off excess egg white from chicken and coat lightly with flour and shake off excess. In wide heavy skillet, over medium high heat, saute chicken in the butter for 4 minutes or just until opaque throughout and golden on both sides. Do not crowd in pan; if necessary, cook only 2 pieces at a time.

Remove to platter and keep warm. Add lemon juice, garlic and ¼ cup water. Cook, stirring, over high heat to loosen crusty drippings and reduce liquid slightly. Add lemon slices to pan and turn in drippings. Pour over chicken, then sprinkle with parsley.

Serves 4.

Ruth Malone

Born in Clarendon, Arkansas, Malone is the author of The Ozark Folk Center Cook Book, *and* Where To Eat in the Ozarks — How It's Cooked.

"Come to my favorite destination — Arkansas! Hunt a diamond at the only diamond mine on the continent. Finders are keepers — from chips to several carats in size. Arkansas, with its white water rapids, unspoiled forests and mountains, hunting and fishing and arts and crafts has something for everyone, young and old, to see and enjoy."

Ruth Malone's Chicken Pie

1 hen (5 pounds)
pastry for top and bottom of casserole
8 medium potatoes, boiled, peeled and diced
8 hard-cooked eggs, diced
1 green pepper, diced

2 tablespoons flour
2 cups rich chicken stock
1 teaspoon salt
$\frac{1}{2}$ teaspoon pepper
1 cup milk

Wash the hen, pat dry and rub salt in cavity and outside. Place the hen in a large heavy pot with cover, add water to within 3 inches of top. Cover and bring water to boil over high heat. Lower heat and simmer chicken until tender, approximately 2 hours (when the leg can be moved back and forth easily, the chicken is done). Let hen cool in broth with lid of pot removed. Skim fat from broth and reserve, saving the broth for sauce. Strip meat from bones, discard gristle and skin, and cut meat into pieces about 2 inches long.

Line a casserole with pastry, saving a circle to cover top of pie. Layer potatoes, eggs, pimento, green pepper and chicken; repeat until all is used to fill casserole, with chicken as the last layer.

Make a paste of flour and a small amount of chicken broth in a saucepan. While stirring over medium heat, gradually add remaining broth, seasonings and the milk. Continue stirring until sauce thickens. Pour gravy, a little at a time, into filled casserole, moving around the casserole as you pour, until it reaches to within a few inches of top.

Place pastry over the chicken-vegetable filling and crimp edges of casserole to seal. Prick pastry in several places to let out steam and spread 1 tablespoon of chicken fat over crust. Bake at 400° until pastry is brown and filling is heated through.

Walter Payton

Born in Columbia, Mississippi, Payton played halfback for the Chicago Bears from 1975 to 1987. He holds the NFL career record for rushing.

Howard D. Simmons

Sweetness Chicken

12 chicken pieces (3 - 3½ pounds)
1½ cups orange juice
2 teaspoons oregano leaves
½ teaspoon garlic powder
½ teaspoon ground sage
½ teaspoon dried rosemary leaves, crushed
½ teaspoon dried thyme, crushed

1 teaspoon salt
¼ teaspoon pepper
paprika
¼ cup orange marmalade
1 tablespoon cornstarch
3 cups cooked rice

Place chicken in 13 x 9-inch baking dish, skin side down. Combine the orange juice and seasonings and pour over chicken. Sprinkle with paprika, cover and bake at 350° for 30 minutes. Turn chicken and sprinkle with paprika. Bake uncovered 30 to 40 minutes longer or until chicken is tender.

Pour pan juices into saucepan and skim fat. Add marmalade and cornstarch dissolved in 2 tablespoons of water. Cook, stirring until sauce is clear and thickened.

Serving Suggestion:
Serve chicken and sauce over bed of rice. Garnish with orange slices.

Makes 6 servings.

Will D. Campbell

Born in Mississippi, Campbell is a minister and award-winning novelist and author of Brother to a Dragonfly *and* Providence.

"The 16th century Anabaptists, the spiritual ancestors of most Mississippians, wouldn't go to war, serve on juries, approve the death penalty or take an oath. So they ate a lot of rabbit. The reason being that they were generally on the run from fellow Christians who burned them to death or drowned them in the Amstel River or Lake Zurich. They weren't in one place long enough to raise chickens, which, incidentally, can be substituted for rabbit if you prefer. Probably they didn't always have all the following ingredients, but they did the best they could."

Anabaptist Rabbit

¼ cup butter (½ stick)
1 large rabbit, cut up
1 large onion, sliced
2 garlic cloves, minced
2 tablespoons flour
½ teaspoon salt
¼ teaspoon pepper

small pinch of basil
2 chicken bouillon cubes
1 cup hot water
20 small new potatoes, cooked
¼ cup red wine
snipped parsley

Saute the rabbit in very hot butter on both sides until well browned. Add onion and garlic and cook for 5 minutes, stirring often.

In a bowl combine flour, salt, pepper and basil. Stir it into the hot water in which the bouillon cubes have been dissolved and pour over the browned rabbit. Cook slowly (covered) 25 to 30 minutes or until rabbit is tender. Add the whole cooked potatoes and wine and heat to serving temperature.

Serving Suggestion:
Garnish with parsley and serve from skillet. The sauce may be doubled if you intend to serve with hot biscuits and are into sopping.

*Chicken can be substituted for rabbit if you prefer.

Donald Harrington

Harrington is recognized as one of the South's major writers. He was born in Little Rock but grew up in the Ozarks and makes his home in Fayetteville. His latest novel, The Choiring of the Trees, *was published in April of 1991 and is one more installment in the* Stay More Saga *which includes* Lightning Bug, The Architecture of the Arkansas Ozarks: A Novel, Some Other Place, The Right Place: A Novel, *and* The Cockroaches of Stay More. *His one work of nonfiction,* Let Us Build Us a City, *was an exploration of 11 Arkansas ghost towns.*

Kim Harrington

"Jasper, Arkansas, the seat of Newton County, is the smallest county seat in Arkansas and one of the smallest in the nation. It is locked into the most spectacular elevations of the Ozark Mountains, a jumping-off place for both the Buffalo National River and for the mythical Stay More County of my novels."

Barbecued Butterflied Leg of Lamb

One leg of lamb, boned

Marinade:
1 cup red wine
½ cup olive oil
⅛ cup tarragon vinegar
⅛ cup lemon juice
1 tablespoon white pepper

1 tablespoon black pepper
1 tablespoon green pepper
1 dozen juniper berries
½ teaspoon rosemary
½ teaspoon thyme
½ teaspoon salt
½ teaspoon mustard

Find a butcher who knows what "butterfly" means. (This is the hard part. Most supermarket butchers do not understand the term, which is basically simple: removing the bone from a leg of lamb so the meat is a flat slab in roughly the shape of papillon.)

Combine ingredients for marinade and pour over the lamb. Marinade for 24 hours or overnight, turning twice.

Skewer the lamb crosswise (X) with skewers to prevent curling. On a stove-top grill (I use Jenn-Air), grill for only 20 minutes per side at medium high setting, and then 6 minutes per side at high setting; or on a charcoal grill, moderate heat, not more than 30 minutes per side.

Total grilling time should not exceed more than 1 hour, and center should remain pink.

James Martin

Born in Savannah, Georgia, Martin served as a member of the U.S. House of Representatives for 12 years before being elected governor of North Carolina in 1984. He is the first Republican elected to two consecutive terms of office in North Carolina history.

"I think North Carolina is unique with such a variety of beautiful scenic attractions. Our family enjoys sailing on our tranquil sounds in the eastern part of the state and equally looks forward to fishing and rafting in our majestic mountains. And unifying all of us are the wonderful, friendly people who call North Carolina home."

Sailboat Chili

1 cup red chili beans
1 cup black beans
4 ounces olive oil
2¼ pounds lamb or beef, diced ½-inch
5 cloves garlic, minced
1 large onion, finely diced
1 red bell pepper, deseeded and finely chopped
3 jalapeno peppers, deseeded and finely chopped
4 cayenne peppers, fresh or dried, deseeded and finely chopped
1 yellow banana pepper, deseeded and finely chopped

8 fresh tomatoes, peeled, deseeded and diced
1 can tomato sauce (29 ounces)
1 can tomato paste (6 ounces)
4 teaspoons cumin
4 teaspoons chili powder
2 teaspoons salt
2 teaspoons tabasco sauce
1 large bay leaf
1 tablespoon fresh oregano, or 1 teaspoon dried
1 tablespoon fresh basil, or 1 teaspoon dried

Wash beans thoroughly. Bring to a boil and simmer approximately 2 hours, or until tender. (This step prevents beans from falling apart). Brown the meat in 2 ounces of olive oil; remove meat and all excess liquid from pan. Place pan back on heat and add remaining 2 ounces of olive oil. Lightly brown garlic, then add onion and brown for approximately 10 minutes. Add all the peppers and continue to cook another 5 minutes. Add diced tomatoes and cook for 10 minutes. Add all remaining ingredients including meat and liquid (except for the beans) and simmer for 45 minutes. After beans are aldente, drain and add to chili.

Makes 10 servings

Joe B. Hall

Born in Cynthiana, Kentucky, Hall is the former head basketball coach at the University of Kentucky.

"My favorite spot to visit in Kentucky is where I grew up, in Harrison and Bourbon counties. I like going back to the streams that I fished as a kid. You go back and the same rocks are there, the same sycamores, the same ripples and bends in the stream — and pretty much the same fish. Not much has changed with those streams, and I've yet to see a hollow sycamore with a TV in it."

Venison or Elk Stew

2 pounds breast or shoulder venison or elk meat
2 tablespoons oil
6 cups boiling water
freshly ground black pepper to taste
2 tablespoons flour

4 medium potatoes, diced
4 carrots, diced
2 turnips, diced
4 onions, diced
seasoned flour

Cut the meat into 1-inch cubes. Roll in seasoned flour and brown in a small amount of oil in a heavy skillet. Add the boiling water and pepper to the browned meat; cover and simmer for 2 to 3 hours.

Add the diced vegetables and cook until tender. Use 2 tablespoons of flour moistened with water to thicken the remaining liquid.

José García

John Folse

Chef and owner of the award-winning LaFitte's Landing Restaurant in Donaldsonville, Louisiana, Folse is also the author of The Encyclopedia of Cajun and Creole Cuisine, *and is respected around the world as an authority on Cajun and Creole cuisine and culture.*

Louisiana Seafood Gumbo

2 pounds of 35-count shrimp, reserve shells
1½ cups oil
1½ cups flour
2 cups onions, chopped
2 cups green onions, chopped; separate and
   reserve greens
1 cup celery, chopped

½ cup bell pepper, chopped
6 pods garlic, chopped
1 pound claw crab meat
1 pound lump crab meat
1 pint oysters, reserve liquor
4 quarts hot water
salt and cayenne to taste

Peel and devein shrimp. In separate pot, boil shrimp shells in 1 quart unseasoned water for 15 to 20 minutes. Strain through cheese cloth and reserve liquid.

In heavy bottom gumbo pot, add oil and flour. Cook over medium high heat stirring constantly until golden brown. Do not scorch. Add all seasonings except green onion tops. Saute for 5 minutes and add the shrimp stock. Add hot water one ladle at a time, until consistency of thick soup is achieved. Add oyster liquor, claw crab meat and ½ of the shrimp. Reduce to simmer and cook approximately 45 minutes stirring occasionally.

Add remaining shrimp, oysters, lump crab meat and green onion tops. Cook 10 to 15 minutes. Season to taste using salt and cayenne pepper. Add water if necessary to retain volume.

Serving Suggestion:
Serve over white rice.

Serves 10.

Sea Captain's House

Originally a summer home with a large porch overlooking a grassy yard and the Atlantic Ocean, the two-story Cape Cod house opened as Sea Captain's House in Myrtle Beach, South Carolina, in 1962.

Philip Rateliff, chef

"One of the most memorable places to visit is in my home state of Arkansas. Eureka Springs, a beautiful mountainside village in northern Arkansas, has many historical buildings and several restored hotels and restaurants still open for business. With nearby Beaver Lake and numerous mountain streams and small rivers for fishing and floating, it is one of the most beautiful and relaxing spots I have ever had the pleasure to visit."

Crab Cakes

2 teaspoons oil
1 medium onion, finely chopped
1 pound lump crab meat; pick off any shell
1½ cups packed fresh white bread crumbs,
    approximately ¼ loaf
3 tablespoons fresh parsley, minced
3 eggs, slightly beaten

1 teaspoon salt
1 teaspoon ground black pepper
1 teaspoon dry mustard
⅙ cup heavy cream
flour to dust cakes
1 stick of butter

Heat medium saute pan over medium high heat. Add 2 teaspoons oil, onion and saute until transparent. Remove from pan into large mixing bowl. Add crab meat, bread crumbs and seasonings, mix until well blended. Chill and shape into 3-ounce cakes (approximately 2½ x 1½ inches thick). Dust lightly with flour.

Place 1 stick butter or vegetable oil in skillet over medium heat. Place crab cakes in hot oil, cook on first side 1½ to 2 minutes, or until lightly browned. Turn and cook 2 minutes on second side. Cakes should be firm in center. Remove from skillet onto paper towel to absorb grease.

Serving suggestion:
Serve with hollandaise sauce or butter with lemon juice, white wine, salt, pepper and dill weed.

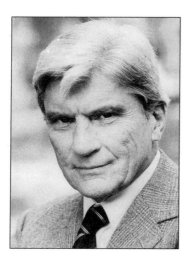

JohnWarner

Born in Washington, D.C., Warner has been a Republican United States senator from Virginia since 1979.

"I would have to say my favorite place to be is in the Old Dominion. With the Senate summer recess there is extra time to travel, and every year I look forward to getting out and seeing my fellow Virginians. There is so much to do and see in the state. From the Tidewater area to the mountainous southwest and from thriving northern Virginia to the serene Shenandoah Valley, we have it all right here in the great commonwealth!"

Norfolk Crab Cakes

Chef's note: This is a creative recipe and the precise measurements, preparation of the mix and cooking variables are trade secrets known only to the chef! Traditional crab cakes are those made with a mix of the ingredients recommended below and amounts to suit the chef's particular taste.

Fresh Chesapeake Bay blue crab meat
   (Important crabs come from the Virginia side
   of the bay!)
fresh onions, preferably at least 2 types for
   variety of flavor and texture
green bell peppers
parsley

vegetable salt
pepper
bread crumbs or a mix with a little cornbread
heavy cream
eggs
fresh butter

Pre-cook onions in butter, taking care not to lose firmness of texture. Slightly saute chopped green bell peppers to release full flavor.
Note: Pre-cooking onions and peppers, then adding cornmeal, if used, at the end of this step reduces the amount of further cooking to which the crab meat is subjected. Crab meat is packaged fully cooked and further heat diminishes its quality.

Mix crab, egg, cooked onions and green peppers, bread crumbs and black pepper.
Note: Crab meat contains the delicate flavors from the "salt sea." Don't try to improve on nature!

Add sufficient cream to bind the mixture lightly. Hand mold the mixture into a cake, no more than $\frac{1}{2}$-to $\frac{3}{4}$-inch thick. Pre-cook the butter. Heat slowly until you see a slight browning of the solids from the butter in the bottom of your pan. Now quickly add the cakes before the butter begins to burn. This takes skillful timing and, once mastered, elevates you to chef!

By now you have had enough of the recipe, especially the advice. Two last hints: The less you have to cook the crab cake, the better, for you are preserving the "seasoning to the sea" and one of nature's finest gifts. When it's done, get it out of the pan; don't let it soak up excess butter.

Good luck, and thank you for making the effort to join me in this venture.

Buddy Roemer

*Born in Shreveport, Louisiana, Roemer served as governor
of Louisiana from 1988 to 1992.*

Crawfish and Noodles

1 bunch green onions, chopped
6 or 7 sprigs parsley, chopped
½ stick butter
1 bunch broccoli, cut in medium-size pieces
instant chicken broth
12 large mushrooms, cut in large pieces
corn starch

¼ cup sherry
1 pound crawfish tails
½ teaspoon white pepper
½ teaspoon Accent
½ cup Parmesan cheese
1 cup sour cream
egg or spinach noodles

Saute green onions and parsley in butter. Add fresh broccoli and small amount of water and cook
for a few minutes. Sprinkle instant chicken broth over broccoli and thicken a bit with corn starch.
Add sherry, crawfish tails, white pepper and Accent. Stir in Parmesan cheese and sour cream.

Serving Suggestion: Serve over egg noodles or spinach noodles.

Serves 4.

Jimmy Carter

Born in Plains, Georgia, Carter was the 39th president of the United States from 1977 to 1981, the first president to be elected from the Deep South since before the Civil War.

After leaving office, former President Jimmy Carter felt an obligation to use the knowledge, influence and experience he gained while in the White House to continue the search for solutions to problems on his national and international agendas. These issues include education, hunger, health, human rights, conflict resolution, environment and the promotion of democracy.

A counsel of distinguished knowledgeable leaders, both here and abroad, led him to develop the Carter Presidential Center. The Center, which was completed in 1986, houses the Jimmy Carter Library, the Carter Center of Emory University, Global 2000 and the Carter-Menil Human Rights Foundation, all of which promote the exploration of important world issues through research, consultations and action.

President Carter's Fried Fish Recipe

fish filets, cut into strips about size of french fries
A-1 or Heinz 57 sauce
Tabasco sauce
Bisquik or pancake mix
peanut oil, or substitute

Marinate fish several hours in A-1 or Heinz 57 sauce with a touch of Tabasco. Shake in bag with Bisquik or pancake mix and deep-fry in peanut oil.

Eat hot or cold.

Cafe Creole

Cafe Creole is located in the heart of Ybor City, the once-glorious center of Tampa, Florida's Spanish-influenced cigar industry. It is located in a historical building called El Pasaje, which originally opened in 1896 as the Cherokee Club, a gentleman's hotel and private club with a casino, restaurant and bar.

Isidro Macho Alfonso, chef
"To ask a man from the South where his favorite place is, is a tough order. Just think about all the great places in our glorious South; such as the thousands of miles of beautiful coastline, countless numbers of winding rivers, near-perfect weather, hunting, fishing, boating, golf. ... I guess you see what I mean. But if I had to come up with one choice it would be a barbecue and beach party on Sunset Beach in St. Petersburg with good friends and family."

Bienville sauce is a classic Creole dressing for baked oysters. This culinary classic has been adapted as a dressing for most any white meat fish and is one of Cafe Creole's most requested dishes!

Grouper Bienville

6 grouper filets (8 ounces), cut ½ inch
¼ cup chopped scallions
¼ pound sliced fresh mushrooms
1 teaspoon chopped garlic
2 tablespoons butter
½ pound medium to small shrimp
1½ teaspoons thyme, whole
1½ teaspoons Old Bay seasoning, or
  any seafood seasoning

⅓ teaspoon white pepper
½ teaspoon Tabasco
1½ teaspoons worcestershire sauce
2 ounces sherry, unsalted
4 tablespoons Romano cheese, grated
2 ounces Monterey Jack cheese, grated
½ pound blue crab meat, claw or lump
¼ cup fresh chopped parsley

Peel and devein shrimp, wash and set aside.

Saute scallions, garlic and mushrooms in butter until soft. Don't over cook. Add shrimp and all seasonings and cook until shrimp are opaque. Add sherry and blend well over high heat for 1 to 2 minutes to cook off alcohol. Add the grated Romano and Monterey Jack cheeses, bechamel sauce, crab meat and fresh parsley. Fold in well. Adjust salt and pepper to taste; let sit until it cools to room temperature.

Spread approximately 4 ounces on each piece of grouper that has been seasoned with salt and pepper. Sprinkle top of dressed grouper with light coating of fine bread crumbs and $\frac{1}{2}$ tablespoon grated Romano cheese. Bake in buttered baking pan at 375° for 30 to 45 minutes, until done and lightly browned on top.

Bechamel Sauce

3 tablespoons butter
3 tablespoons flour
$1\frac{1}{4}$ cups warm milk

In small saute pan, melt butter and wisk in flour. When flour is well blended, add warm milk and cook over medium heat until thick. Set aside until ready to fold into seafood mixture.

Nick Kelsh

Billy Joe Tatum

Born in Little Rock, Arkansas, Tatum is the author of Billy Joe Tatum's Wild Foods Field Guide and Cook Book.

"Crisp autumn air, subtle color transformation of leaves, the burst of purple and gold fall asters and goldenrod — all an invitation to float and fish the White River. Putting in at Allison in Stone County, Arkansas, and leisurely floating to Guion in Izard County is a great way to sample the season, catch trout and enjoy a superb meal cooked and savored on a gravel bar while anticipating sighting of an eagle, mink, deer or wild turkey, also perhaps, savoring the season."

Trout Stuffed with Cedar Berries

2 rainbow trout, gutted, washed and rubbed with salt inside and out
2 onions, sliced thinly into rings
2 lemons, sliced into thin circles
3 tablespoons herbs of your choice (basil, thyme, fennel, dill, marjoram)

1 cup cedar or juniper berries
oil or butter
foil for wrapping or tightly covered iron skillet or dutch oven

Mix cedar berries with half the onions and 2 tablespoons herbs. Stuff cavity of fish with mixture and add several slices of lemon. Rub outside of fish with oil. Place half the remaining onion rings and lemon slices on foil. Lay fish on foil and cover with remaining lemon and onion. Sprinkle with herbs and wrap foil tightly around the fish. Cook over grill or open fire or in a covered iron skillet about 20 minutes or until the fish falls off the bone. Remove stuffing and serve.

Deborah Norville

Born in Dalton, Georgia, Norville is the former co-anchor of NBC News' "Today" and is currently hosting a talk show for ABC radio.

"My favorite destination is a little spot one must hike to within the White River National Forest in northeast Georgia. I won't tell you how to get there or it won't be a 'secret' anymore. But take this tip to visit off the beaten path — that's where the real treasures are!"

Cajun Shrimp

with thanks to Paul Prudhomme

2 sticks unsalted butter
$\frac{1}{2}$ cup finely chopped green onions (tops only)
1 teaspoon minced garlic
1 pound shrimp, peeled
2 teaspoons Chef Paul Prudhomme's Seafood Magic®

$\frac{1}{4}$ teaspoon dry mustard
1 teaspoon Tabasco sauce
$1\frac{1}{2}$ cups hot cooked rice

Heat serving plates in a 250° oven. Place 1 stick of butter, the onions and garlic in a large skillet. Saute 1 minute over high heat. Add shrimp and seasonings and saute over high heat for 3 minutes, stirring occasionally. Break remaining butter into chunks and add to pan. Continue cooking over high heat for 6 minutes, shaking pan constantly. Serve immediately.

Serving Suggestion:
Mound $\frac{1}{2}$ cup rice in middle of each heated serving plate. Encircle the rice with 1 cup sauteed shrimp and sauce.

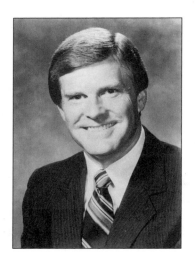

CarrollA. Campbell, Jr.

Born in Greenville, South Carolina, Campbell served as a Republican congressman from 1979 until he was elected governor of South Carolina in 1987.

LowCountryShrimpandSausage

2 pounds fresh medium-size shrimp
2 pounds Italian sausage
3 green bell peppers
3 medium onions

3 tablespoons oil
1 ounce Zatarain's Creole seasoning mix or
   cajun spice

Peel and devein shrimp, wash and set aside.

Place sausage in 425° oven until well cooked, about 30 to 40 minutes. Remove the sausage, cut into ½-inch pieces and set aside. Cut onions and peppers into strips and saute in 3 tablespoons of oil, cooking until half done. Add shrimp, sausage and cajun seasoning, stirring frequently until shrimp is done. Remove from heat and serve immediately.

Serving Suggestion: Campbell says: "We usually serve it with grits, a Southern favorite."

CarrollAngelle

Born in Cecilia, St. Martin Parish, Louisiana, Angelle is an award-winning chef and restaurant owner.

ShrimpEtouffee

1 onion, chopped
½ bell pepper, chopped
1 stick margarine
salt
pepper
cayenne pepper

paprika
2 pounds peeled shrimp
½ cup flour
1½ cups water
½ bunch green onions, chopped

Saute onion and bell pepper in margarine. Add salt and peppers to taste, along with 2 or 3 dashes of paprika. Cook for 15 to 20 minutes over medium heat. Add shrimp and stir for about 5 minutes. Add flour and stir for 3 to 5 minutes. Add water and cook 15 to 20 minutes.

Serving Suggestion:
Serve over rice and top with green onions.

Bud Dunn

John Jakes

Born in Chicago, Illinois, but now residing on Hilton Head Island, South Carolina, Jakes is the author of The Bastard *and* The Rebels.

"The region presents many a desirable destination for a history buff. The Virginia battlefields, for example. But I would have to single out Fort Sumter in Charleston's harbor, because of the epochal events touched off by what happened there in 1861."

Shrimp in Wine Sauce, Low Country Style

3 tablespoons butter	2 tablespoons brandy or cognac
1 chopped green onion	¾ cup dry white wine
1½ pounds cleaned shrimp	1 cup milk
pinch of thyme	1 whole egg
bay leaf	1 teaspoon lemon juice
salt and pepper	1 tablespoon parsley, chopped

Saute the onion in butter and add the shrimp and spices; simmer 4 to 5 minutes. Heat the brandy, ignite and pour over shrimp. Stir with an unburnable spoon until flame dies. Remove the shrimp to a warm platter and continue cooking the pan liquid until half reduced. Mix the remaining ingredients and add to pan. Stir until just thickened. Immediately pour the hot thickened sauce over shrimp on platter.

Sea Captain's House

Originally a summer home with a large porch overlooking a grassy yard and the Atlantic Ocean, the two-story Cape Cod house opened as Sea Captain's House in Myrtle Beach, South Carolina, in 1962.

Philip Rateliff, chef

"Another favorite Southern destination of mine is Jacksonville, Florida. Jacksonville has a progressive urban area, offering all the attraction and conveniences of a large city. Just across the intracoastal waterway are Jacksonville's beaches, one of the best places I know to unwind."

Seafarer's Omelette

2 eggs, beaten
4 mushrooms, washed, sliced and sauted in small amount of oil
1 teaspoon green onion tops, chopped
1 ounce Monterey Jack cheese, grated
5 shrimp
¾ ounce lump crab meat

Tobasco sauce
worchestershire sauce
salt and white pepper
1 lemon wedge
2 teaspoons salt
½ teaspoon black pepper
2 cups water

In small saucepan with 2 cups boiling water, add 1 lemon wedge, 2 teaspoons salt and ½ teaspoon black pepper. Add shrimp and cook for 4 minutes. Remove shrimp from water and immerse immediately in ice water to stop cooking process. Peel and devein, set aside.

In small non-aluminum bowl, put eggs, 4 drops worchestershire sauce, 3 drops Tobasco, salt and white pepper. Beat with fork to blend and add remaining ingredients; mix well.

Heat non-stick omelette pan (8 inch) over medium heat. Add ½ teaspoon melted butter, margarine, or non-stick spray. Pour egg mixture into pan. As eggs begin to set, pull edge of omelette towards center of pan, allowing uncooked egg to run into exposed area of pan by tilting pan. Cook for 2 minutes on first side. Flip with non-metal spatula (to avoid scratching pan) and cook on second side for 3 minutes, or until center is firm. Fold over halfway and slide out onto plate.

Serving Suggestion:
Garnish with fresh fruit or chilled sliced tomatoes.

Yields one portion.

John Sherman Cooper

Born in Somerset, Kentucky, Cooper was a United Nations delegate in 1949-51 and 1968-81. He is the former ambassador to India, Nepal and East Germany. He died in 1990 at the age of 89.

Eggs Somerset

2 cups crab meat or lobster
½ cup butter
pinch of salt
½ cup heavy cream
dash of red pepper
dash of paprika

dash of nutmeg
3 eggs, beaten
3 tablespoons sherry
6 eggs, poached
Gruyère cheese
1½ - 2 cups white sauce

Cook crab meat, butter and salt slowly for 3 minutes in double boiler. Add cream, red pepper, paprika and nutmeg and heat thoroughly. Add beaten eggs and cook until thickened. Just before removing from fire add sherry and put mixture in casserole dish.

Poach 6 eggs until yellows are almost firm and place on top. Dot generously with Gruyère cheese and cover with white sauce. Place in oven at 500° until mixture is brown and bubbly, about 25 minutes.

Serving Suggestion:
Garnish with puff pastry.

White Sauce

4 tablespoons butter
4 tablespoons flour
2 cups milk

Melt butter in saucepan and stir in flour until smooth. Slowly add milk and stir constantly over medium heat until thickened.

Theodore Taylor

Born in Statesville, North Carolina, Taylor is the author of several books for young adults and adults including People Who Make Movies, The Cay, The Magnificent Mitscher *and* The Stalker.

"My favorite destinations in North Carolina are the Blue Ridge Mountains in the spring and fall, the Hatteras coast in the late summer — places where I spent time as a boy, in days when life was rather slow and gentle. In Virginia, the Tidewater area — Portsmouth, Norfolk and Newport News. Again, boyhood memories of the Elizabeth River and Hampton Roads, my own boat and explorations on water."

Gin Fizz Egg Pie

6 strips thick bacon
1 onion, diced
1 can peeled tomatoes (28 ounces)
10 fresh mushrooms, sliced
2 cans Vienna sausages, cut into 1/4-inch slices
6 slices Jack or American cheese

1 dozen eggs
1/2 cup fresh cream
Parmesan cheese
pimento strips
sour cream
a shaker of gin fizzes

Cut bacon into 1-inch pieces; fry until crisp in a large skillet. Pour off most of grease; brown onions in rest. Mix in tomatoes, mushrooms and Vienna sausages; let simmer 15 minutes. During last minutes, stir in cheese slices.

Gently beat eggs with cream and stir into pan mixture. Bake at 350° for 30 minutes or until eggs have cooked to a nice golden crust. For last 5 minutes, sprinkle Parmesan cheese over crust.

Serving Suggestions:
Mix a shaker of gin fizzes on entry of pan into oven, and enjoy, enjoy until eggs are done. Serve eggs in pie slices, garnished with thin strips of pimento on each slice and a bowl of sour cream for those who desire this final touch.

Vegetables & Side Dishes

CarrollAngelle

Born in Cecilia, St. Martin Parish, Louisiana, Angelle is an award-winning chef and restaurant owner.

SmotheredCabbage

2 heads of cabbage, sliced, not too fine
1 medium bell pepper, chopped
1 large onion, chopped
1 cup vegetable oil
salt and pepper to taste
1 pound ham, cubed
¼ cup sugar

In a heavy pot, place oil, cabbage, bell pepper, onion, salt and pepper. Cook over medium heat, covered, for 30 minutes. Add ham and cook for an additional 30 minutes. Add sugar and let cook, uncovered, until cabbage is golden brown. Stir occasionally.

Umm — c'est bon!

Alex Haley

Born in Henning, Tennessee, Haley is the author of Roots, *the Pulitzer Prize-winning novel which had the largest hard cover printing in U.S. publishing history. "Roots," the mini-series, became the most-watched dramatic show in television history.*

"My favorite destination is Knoxville, Tennessee, nowadays, with apologies to the small town of Henning, Tennessee, which I love as my boyhood hometown. After having traveled a good deal of the world in connection with having been 20 years in the U.S. Coast Guard and then writing Roots, *I lived for a time in New York and then in Beverly Hills, and what brought me solace, finally, was moving back home — to Tennessee, and to Knoxville because I fell in love with the east Tennessee people and topography. Now I have a home in Knoxville and a beautiful farm about 25 miles to the north, so traveling man that I am, my favorite destination is Knoxville."*

Corn Pudding

10 ears of corn	3 egg yolks, beaten
3 tablespoons butter	3 tablespoons sugar, optional
2 tablespoons all-purpose flour	1 teaspoon salt
1 pint milk	3 egg whites, beaten until stiff

Cut and shave corn from cobs. Melt butter and smooth flour in it. Add milk, beaten yolks, sugar and salt. Fold in egg whites. Bake in greased casserole dish at 350° for 45 minutes or until firm.

Ellen Douglass

Emily Haxton

Novelist and short story writer, Douglass has been the winner of the Houghton Mifflin Esquire Fellowship Award and the Mississippi Institute of Arts and Letters Literature Award.

"I am not much of a traveler. I love rural south Mississippi where I was born and where a son and daughter-in-law and grandchildren live.

"Cushaws are giant crook-necked members of the squash family. They are available in farmers' markets and occasionally in supermarkets in the late summer and fall. They will keep for several months if stored in a cool dry place. Tradition has it that the first seeds were brought to this country from Africa by slaves. The first ones I ate as a child came from seeds handed down season by season in the family of a very old black man whom I knew in Adams County. In his honor I call this recipe 'Henry Davis' Baked Cushaw.'"

Henry Davis' Baked Cushaw

6 cups cushaw flesh (1 cushaw)
1 stick melted butter or margarine
1 cup sugar
1 teaspoon freshly grated nutmeg

Cut the cushaw in large pieces, using a cleaver if the skin is very tough. Scrape out the seeds and discard. Boil the flesh until tender, approximately 20 to 40 minutes; test with a fork.

Allow to cool and drain thoroughly in colander. Peel and discard skin. Mix and mash the flesh together with the remaining ingredients. Spread in several shallow baking dishes or pie pans and bake in 300° oven for about 1½ hours or longer, depending on how well drained the cushaw flesh was. When done, the cushaw begins to brown on top and caramelize slightly around the edges.

Serving Suggestions:
Serve as a side dish with ham or pork roast. The finished casseroles freeze well and can be thawed and reheated for 30 minutes or so.

Susan Johann

Marsha Norman

Born in Louisville, Kentucky, Norman won the 1983 Pulitzer Prize in drama for 'Night Mother, *which was made into a movie in 1986. Her work is characterized by honesty and natural dialogue.*

"After all these years, my favorite places to visit are still the two places I loved best as a child growing up in Kentucky: Shakertown at Pleasant Hill, for its elegance, its staff and its Shaker lemon pie; and Mammoth Cave, for its awe-inspiring silliness. Right this moment, I would give anything to have my guide turn out the lights and direct me to look behind me at the shadow portrait of Martha Washington on the wall."

Cheese Grits Souffle

1 cup quick grits	1 1/2 cups grated Cheddar cheese
1 teaspoon salt	1 stick butter
1/2 teaspoon garlic powder	2 cups water
2 eggs	2 cups milk

Bring water and milk to boil. Add quick grits, salt and garlic powder; cook according to directions on box. When thick, remove from heat and add butter and cheese. Stir until melted. Add slightly beaten eggs and stir. Pour into greased casserole and bake at 350° for 1 hour or until brown.

Willard Scott

Born in Alexandria, Virginia, Scott has been the weathercaster on NBC's "Today Show" since 1980.

"As to a favorite Southern destination in my travels, it would be impossible for me to make such a selection. ... I love them all!"

Cheese Grits Souffle

1 cup quick-cooking grits
4½ cups water
2 teaspoons salt
⅓ cup butter
1 stick Kraft garlic cheese or Kraft Cheddar
   cheese
2 eggs, beaten

¼ cup milk
¼ teaspoon pepper

Topping (optional):
1 cup crushed corn flakes
¼ stick butter

Cook grits in water with 1 teaspoon salt. When done, stir in butter and cheese and allow to cool. Combine eggs and milk and season with salt and pepper. Mix with grits and pour into buttered casserole dish. Mix corn flakes and butter and cover top of casserole. Cover and bake 40 to 45 minutes at 350°.

Nathalie Dupree

Dupree, a native of Georgia, is one of America's hottest cooking sensations. She is a renowned cookbook author, columnist and television star with several top-rated television series and best-selling books to her credit, including New Southern Cooking, Nathalie Dupree's Matters of Taste *and* Nathalie Dupree Cooks for Family & Friends.

"My favorite destination would be 'Nathalie's,' at the Richmond Marriott. It is the first of what Marriott hopes will be many dining establishments featuring my recipes."

Grits with Cream

½ cup quick grits
2 cups heavy cream
2-3 tablespoons butter
salt

freshly ground white pepper
½ cup freshly grated Parmesan, Swiss or
    Monterey Jack cheese

Cook grits according to package directions, substituting cream for water. Stir occasionally, being careful they do not burn. If grits begin to separate and turn lumpy, add water to keep them creamy. When done, remove from heat, and add the butter, salt and pepper to taste. Stir in the cheese and serve.

This may be made ahead and reheated over low heat or in a microwave.

Mitch McConnell

Born in Colbert County, Alabama, and raised in Louisville, Kentucky, McConnell, a Republican, has been a United States senator from Kentucky since 1984.

"Your question regarding my favorite place to visit in the 11 Southern states is both difficult and simple. Since I live in Washington, D.C., most of the year, those trips I make to Kentucky are always the most enjoyable. The difficulty lies in which part of Kentucky I find the most intriguing. From the mountains of eastern Kentucky to the rolling farmlands of western Kentucky, from the metropolitan atmosphere of Louisville to the horse farms of Lexington, each place holds a special place in my heart."

Hoppin' John

2 cups fresh or frozen black-eyed peas
$1/4$ pound slab bacon
2 small pods red peppers
$1/2$ cup uncooked regular rice
salt to taste

In a pot, cover peas with water. Add salt and pepper to taste. Add bacon and peppers and simmer over low heat for 1 to $1^1/2$ hours, until tender. Add rice, cover and cook over low heat, stirring frequently until rice is cooked.

Add more water during cooking if necessary.

Geoffrey Beene

*Born in Haynesville, Louisiana, Beene is an award-winning
fashion designer.*

*"My favorite spot in the South is where I spent so many
pleasant hours after hours during my medical studies at
Tulane University in New Orleans. It is Cafe du Monde or
'morning call' in the French Quarter. It has a delightful
casual ambiance all 24 hours, with superb architectural
views of the city and, of course, that of the great Mississippi River. Unique and grand!"*

Lucille's Dirty Rice

1 stick margarine
½ cup onion, chopped
½ cup celery, chopped
½ cup green pepper, chopped
1 can mushroom soup

1 can beef consommé
1 cup water
1 cup rice
½ teaspoon salt

Preheat oven to 375°. Saute onions, celery and peppers in margarine. Mix all ingredients together
and place in casserole. Cover and bake 1 hour, stirring occasionally.

Rufus Thomas

Internationally acclaimed entertainer, Thomas was born in Memphis, Tennessee.

"I was born in the country, raised in town, and can watcha shake it from my hips on down! As ambassador to Memphis, my favorite destination has to be Memphis and its legendary Beale Street — Home of the Blues."

Famous Macaroni and Cheese

1 package elbow macaroni (8 ounces)
3 tablespoons butter
1 cup milk
¼ teaspoon salt

¼ teaspoon black pepper
2 eggs, beaten
12 ounces shredded Cheddar cheese

Bring water to boil in 3-quart saucepan. Add package of macaroni, stirring constantly until tender. Remove from fire and rinse in collander with cold water. Use 1½ tablespoons of butter to cover bottom and sides of casserole dish. Place half the macaroni in dish and cover with half of the Cheddar cheese, sprinkle with salt and pepper. Add the remainder of macaroni. In mixing bowl, combine eggs and milk and beat until mixed. Pour over macaroni and cheese mixture, sprinkling balance of salt and pepper. Top with remaining Cheddar cheese and pour 1½ tablespoons of melted butter over casserole. Bake in a 375° oven for 25 minutes.

Minnie Pearl

Born in Centerville, Tennessee, Pearl is a country music performer whose trademark is a straw hat with the price tag hanging on it. She has appeared on TV's "Hee Haw" and was inducted into the Country Music Hall of Fame in 1975.

"After so much traveling (50 years) I just love to stay home in beautiful Nashville!"

Macaroni and Cheese

1/2 pound sharp cheese
1/4 cup butter or margarine
1/4 cup all-purpose flour
1 chicken bouillon cube, crushed
1/2 teaspoon onion powder
1/4 teaspoon white pepper
1 1/2 teaspoons seasoned salt
1/4 teaspoon dry mustard
dash of cayenne pepper
dash of ground nutmeg
2 cups milk
8 ounces macaroni, cooked
paprika

Preheat oven to 350°. Grease shallow 2-quart baking dish.

Cut cheese in 1/2-inch cubes. Melt butter in saucepan. Add flour, bouillon cube and seasonings. Cook over low heat, stirring frequently, until mixture is bubbly. Stir in milk and cook until sauce is thick. Add 1 cup cheese cubes and stir until melted. Remove from heat.

Place half of macaroni in prepared baking dish. Sprinkle with half of remaining cheese. Repeat. Pour sauce over top. Sprinkle generously with paprika. Bake 30 to 35 minutes.

Serves 6.

Cheesy New Potatoes

12 medium new potatoes
1 cup medium-sharp cheese, grated
8 slices bacon, cooked and crumbled
1/2 cup melted butter or margarine
salt and pepper to taste

Wash potatoes, but don't peel. Slice into 1/4-inch slices. Cook in boiling salted water until done.

Preheat oven to 400°. Grease a 2-quart casserole dish. Place layer each of potatoes, cheese and bacon in casserole dish. Pour on half the butter. Sprinkle with salt and pepper. Repeat. Heat in oven about 15 minutes.

Serves 8.

Eudora Welty

Born in Jackson, Mississippi, Welty is an author who won a 1972 Pulitzer Prize for The Optimist's Daughter.

"This is from a recipe Katherine Anne Porter gave me, which she got in France. These little pies are served hot at the wine festivals along with a bottle of wine."

Onion Pie

Crust:
A lump of butter size of an egg, 3 tablespoons
1 rounded teaspoon lard
1 heaping teaspoon baking powder
salt
1 heaping cup of flour (sift before measuring)
3 tablespoons cold sweet milk
1 egg yolk, optional

Filling:
3 large sweet Spanish onions, shaved finely
1 large tablespoon butter
1 teaspoon flour
salt and pepper
2 eggs, beaten
1 cup whipping cream

Work together the softened butter, lard, baking powder, salt and flour. Add enough cold, sweet milk to make a good firm dough; a well-beaten yolk of an egg may be added if desired. Line an 8-inch pie plate with rolled pastry.

Fry onions in butter until nicely browned and reduced. Add flour and stir well. Add salt and pepper to taste. Mix eggs until light and add cream. Fold into onions gently until perfectly mixed. Pour into crust and bake at 400° for about 30 minutes or till brown and puffy.

Serves 4.

The Statler Brothers

A country harmony group from Staunton, Virginia, with many hit singles since the early 1960s, the group consists of Philip Balsley, Lew C. DeWitt, Don S. Reid and Harold W. Reid.

"We love the South and all her states, but we have a loving leaning toward Virginia. It's home to all four of us. Home is always the most appealing destination after a long tour.

"Virginia is a warm sight in any season. Whether we're heading back for our annual Fourth of July celebration in our hometown, Staunton, or whether we're just 'going home' for a few days, it's a nice place to nestle."

Potato Casserole

2 pounds frozen hashbrowns, thawed
½ cup melted butter
¼ to ½ teaspoon salt
½ cup chopped onion
1 pint sour cream
1 can cream of chicken soup
2 cups Cheddar cheese, grated

Topping:
2 cups corn flakes, crushed
¼ cup melted butter
or:
one can of Durkee's onions

Preheat oven to 350°. Mix all casserole ingredients together. Bake in greased 9 x 15-inch glass dish at 350° for 15 to 20 minutes. Mix topping ingredients, place on top of casserole and bake an additional 5 to 10 minutes, until bubbling and brown.

Ronnie Milsap

Born in Robbinsville, North Carolina, Milsap is a country music performer whose hit songs have included "Almost Like A Song," "Smoky Mountain Rain" and "Any Day Now."

"My favorite destination, naturally, is North Carolina. That's where I was born and raised, and just getting the opportunity to visit my home area at the foot of the Smokies always gives me an inner peace and perspective I don't seem to get anywhere else in the world. I made the statement in my autobiography that 'memories never die in the mountains,' and that's right ... they don't!"

Stir-Fry American Style

1 ½ cups carrots, thinly sliced
1 ½ cups zucchini, sliced
½ cup onion, chopped
⅓ cup squeeze Parkay margarine
1 can bean sprouts, drained (16 ounces)

1 can water chestnuts, drained and halved (8 ounces)
1 jar whole mushrooms, drained (4 ½ ounces)
1 teaspoon salt
¾ cup Kraft grated Parmesan cheese

Saute carrots, zucchini and onion in margarine in large skillet until lightly browned. Stir occasionally. Add bean sprouts, water chestnuts, mushrooms and salt and heat thoroughly, stirring constantly. Remove from heat and toss lightly with cheese.

Serving suggestion: Top with additional cheese if desired.

Makes 6 servings.

Joe Frank Harris

Born in Cartersville, Georgia, Harris was governor of Georgia from 1983 to 1990.

"My favorite destination is the North Georgia mountains, equally as beautiful in the spring with the dogwood and native plants blooming through the summer and fall, when the color is at its peak. Golfing, fishing in the mountain streams, hiking or skiing in the winter months provides a variety of outdoor activity and sightseeing pleasure throughout the year."

Georgia Sweet Potato Souffle

3 cups mashed sweet potatoes
1½ cups sugar
3 eggs
½ cup milk
1¼ stick butter or margarine

½ teaspoon salt
1 teaspoon vanilla
¾ cup brown sugar
¾ cup self-rising flour
½ to 1 cup chopped pecans

Combine sweet potatoes, sugar, eggs, milk, ½ stick butter, salt and vanilla and pour the mixture into a baking dish. Mix the brown sugar, flour, ¾ stick butter and pecans by hand until blended. Spread the topping on potato mixture and bake until topping is browned, about 25 to 30 minutes in a 350° oven.

Randy Travis

Born in Marshville, North Carolina, Travis is a country music performer whose first number one single was "Forever and Ever, Amen" in 1987. Other hits include "It's Just a Matter of Time" and "1982." He has won several awards in the country music industry.

"I have traveled all over the country touring and I would have to say my home in Tennessee is my favorite destination. I seldom get the chance to be home and I enjoy riding my horses on my farm in Cheatham County."

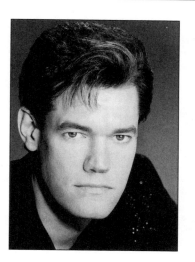

Sweet Potato Casserole

3 cups cooked mashed sweet potatoes
1 cup sugar
2 eggs
1 teaspoon vanilla
⅓ cup milk
½ cup butter or margarine

Topping:
1 cup brown sugar, firmly packed
⅓ cup all-purpose flour
⅓ cup butter or margarine
1 cup finely chopped pecans

Combine sweet potatoes, sugar, eggs, vanilla, milk and ½ cup butter. Beat with electric mixer until smooth. Spoon into a greased 2-quart shallow casserole. Combine topping ingredients and sprinkle over top of casserole. Bake at 350° for 30 minutes.

Serves 8 to 10.

❦ Desserts

Richard Petty

Born in Level Cross, North Carolina, Petty is an auto racer who has won more Grand National stock car races than any other driver. He announced his retirement in 1991.

"Our race team travels several thousand miles during the year to approximately 12 different states. I guess my favorite destination is always the trip back home."

Angel Food Cake

1½ cups egg whites
1 teaspoon cream of tartar
1½ cups sugar

1 teaspoon vanilla
¼ teaspoon salt
1 cup sifted flour, sifted 4 times

Beat egg whites until foamy, add cream of tartar and beat until stiff but not dry. Gradually beat in sugar. Add salt and vanilla. Fold in flour as gently as possible. Bake in angel food pan at 325° for 1 hour and 15 minutes or until top is nicely browned.

Guy Hunt

Born in Holly Pond, Alabama, Hunt, a Republican, was elected governor of Alabama in 1987.

"Regarding my favorite place to visit, I am most fond of vacationing in Gulf Shores. Located on Alabama's Gulf Coast, Gulf Shores has everything you're looking for in a vacation spot with its miles of sparkling white beaches, blue Gulf water and sports for all interests."

Fresh Apple Cake

2 cups sugar
1¼ cups Mazola oil
4 eggs
3 cups flour
1 cup pecans

½ teaspoon salt
1 teaspoon soda
1 teaspoon vanilla
3 cups chipped apples
1 cup coconut

Beat sugar, oil and eggs and add flour and mix. Add the vanilla, pecans, coconut and apples.

Bake in tube pan at 350° for 1 hour to 1 hour 15 minutes.

Remove from pan when cool. Let set, wrapped in foil for a day. Cake moistens as it sets. Freezes well.

Frank Hickingbotham

Born in McGehee, Arkansas, Hickinbotham is the chairman and founder of TCBY Enterprises, Inc.

"Colorful New Orleans, known for its good food and streets that never sleep, has to be one of my favorite destinations. The city is alive: It's filled with legend and history that come together in an exciting blend of cultures. You can see it in the people, hear it in the voices and taste it in the food. Just to visit New Orleans is to put a finger on the pulse of its personality.

"Another favorite of mine is TCBY frozen yogurt. And, in the following recipe, it forms the base for a delicious cocoa raspberry cake that crowns any meal. This recipe is taken from the 'TCBY and More' recipe book."

Cocoa Raspberry Cake

1 ¼ cups plus ⅓ cup TCBY frozen raspberry
  yogurt, divided
2 ⅓ cups all-purpose flour
⅔ cup unsweetened cocoa powder
1 teaspoon salt
½ teaspoon baking powder

¼ teaspoon baking soda
1 ½ cup butter or margarine, softened
3 cups granulated sugar
2 teaspoons vanilla
5 eggs
1 ½ cups confectioners sugar, sifted

Thaw yogurt by placing it in refrigerator overnight. Shake or mix before using if normal separation occurs during thawing.

Preheat oven to 325°. Grease and flour 12-cup bundt pan or 10-inch tube pan and set aside.

Sift flour, cocoa, salt, baking powder and baking soda. Beat butter and granulated sugar in large bowl until light and fluffy. Beat in vanilla. Add eggs, one at a time, beating well after each addition. Add flour-cocoa mixture to butter mixture alternately with 1 ¼ cups yogurt and beat until blended (refrigerate remaining yogurt until ready to use).

Pour batter into prepared pan and smooth top. Bake for 1 hour 10 minutes and cool in pan on wire rack for 15 minutes. Remove from pan and cool completely on rack.

Place reserved ⅓ cup yogurt in small bowl. Add the confectioners sugar and beat vigorously with wire whisk until smooth. Refrigerate for 45 minutes, stir glaze well and spoon or drizzle over top of cooled cake. Refrigerate until ready to serve.

Serves 12 to 16.

Naomi Judd

Born in Ashland, Kentucky, Judd is the mother in the mother-daughter country duo The Judds, whose hits include "Love Can Build a Bridge," "Grandpa (Tell Me About the Good Old Days)" and "Mama He's Crazy."

Coconut Cake

1 box white cake mix
2 cups sour cream
2 cups sugar
2 cups coconut
½ teaspoon almond extract

Make cake following directions on box to make 2 layers. When the cake is cooled, split each layer making a total of 4 layers.

Mix the sour cream and sugar thoroughly. Add the coconut and the almond extract and mix well. Spread between the layers and on the top and sides of the cake. Refrigerate overnight. The cake must be kept refrigerated.

Orange Ice

1 quart water
2 cups sugar
2 cups unsweetened orange juice
¼ cup lemon juice

Boil the water and sugar for 15 minutes, let cool. Add the orange juice and lemon juice and place in freezer. When the mixture is mushy remove and beat thoroughly. Refreeze.

If you use fresh-squeezed oranges, scoop out the left-over pulp and serve the orange ice in the cleaned-out shell.

Bart Starr

Born in Montgomery, Alabama, Starr was the quarterback for the Green Bay Packers in 1956-71. He set several NFL passing records, was voted Most Valuable Player in the 1967 and 1968 Super Bowls and was inducted into the Football Hall of Fame in 1977.

"My favorite destination today is Nashville, Tennessee. It is a beautiful city with its rolling hills, beautiful historic homes, warm, loving people and Civil War history. But I go there frequently because my favorite two little people live there, my granddaughters, Shannon and Jennifer Starr."

Coconut Pecan Cake

½ cup margarine
½ cup shortening
2 cups sugar
5 eggs, separated
1 teaspoon vanilla
2 cups all-purpose flour, sifted

1 teaspoon soda
½ teaspoon salt
1 cup buttermilk
1 can flaked coconut (3½ ounces)
1 cup chopped pecans

Cream margarine and shortening until light and fluffy. Add 1½ cups sugar gradually; beat again until light and fluffy. Add egg yolks and vanilla; beat thoroughly. Add flour sifted with soda and salt in thirds alternately with buttermilk, beating until smooth after each addition. Turn batter into a 3-quart mixing bowl.

Beat egg whites until stiff but not dry. Beat remaining ½ cup sugar into egg whites gradually. Fold egg whites into batter gently but thoroughly. Fold in coconut and pecans.

Bake at 375° for approximately 45 minutes, or until brown.

Serving Suggestions:
Fill and frost as desired. We use a boiled icing with additional coconut. Whipped cream also recommended.

Makes 12 to 16 servings.

Keith Perry

B. B. King

Born in Indianola, Mississippi, King is an internationally known blues singer. With over 50 albums to his name, the international "King of the Blues" still loves the South.

"I claim both Indianola, Mississippi, and Memphis, Tennessee, as my home. I was born on a plantation in Indianola and my career was launched in Memphis. Both places are rich in music heritage and famous for their down-home cooking."

B. B.'s German Chocolate Double Delight

4 ounces German sweet chocolate
1 cup butter
4 egg yolks, unbeaten
2½ cups cake flour
1 teaspoon baking soda
4 egg whites, stiffly beaten

½ cup boiling water
2 cups sugar
1 teaspoon vanilla
½ teaspoon salt
1 cup buttermilk

Melt the chocolate in boiling water and let cool. Cream the butter and sugar until fluffy. Add egg yolks, one at a time, and beat well after each addition. Add the melted chocolate and vanilla; mix well. Sift flour, salt and baking soda and add alternately with buttermilk to chocolate mixture, beating until smooth after each addition. Fold in the beaten egg whites. Pour into three 8- or 9-inch layer pans lined with paper and bake at 350° for 30 to 40 minutes. Cool and frost middle and top only with coconut-pecan frosting.

Coconut-Pecan Frosting

1 cup evaporated milk
1 cup sugar
3 egg yolks
½ cup butter or margarine

1 teaspoon vanilla
1⅓ cups coconut, shredded
1 cup chopped pecans

In saucepan, combine milk, sugar, egg yolks, butter and vanilla. Cook over medium heat stirring constantly, until thickened. Add coconut and pecans, and beat until thick enough to spread.

Makes 2½ cups.

Holly Hunter

Born in Conyers, Georgia, Hunter was nominated for an Acadamy Award for her role in Broadcast News, *for which she was named Best Actress by the New York Film Critics in 1988. She also starred in* Always *and* Raising Arizona.

"My favorite destination in the South is Conyers, Georgia, to my family's farm — where I was born and grew up. This cake recipe is the only recipe I carry everywhere with me in my address book, so I can whip it up at a moment's notice. It's always been a 'must' for all birthdays and celebrations."

Little Wonder Chocolate Cake

2 cups sugar
6 heaping tablespoons cocoa
1 pinch salt
2 egg yolks
6 tablespoons melted butter

1 cup buttermilk
2 level teaspoons baking soda
$2\frac{1}{4}$ cups cake flour
1 cup hot water
1 teaspoon vanilla

Mix the sugar, cocoa and salt and add the egg yolks; mix well. Add melted butter and mix well. Measure the baking soda into the buttermilk and stir until buttermilk foams into a batter. Pour into the mixture. Add the flour and mix well. Add the hot water and vanilla and mix until smooth. Pour the batter into a greased and floured tube pan and bake for 45 minutes at 325°.

Bill Clinton

Born in Hope, Arkansas, Clinton is the Democratic governor of Arkansas and a presidential candidate in 1992.

"A favorite destination is a trip to Hot Springs National Park, Arkansas, which features numerous historic structures open for tour to include the National Historic Landmark known as Bathhouse Row built around world-famous thermal mineral spring waters. Beautiful mountains, sparkling lakes and landmark attractions make the Spa City an enjoyable excursion."

Pound Cake

1 pound butter
3 cups sugar
6 eggs

1 teaspoon vanilla
3½ cups flour
1 cup buttermilk

Preheat oven to 350°, grease and flour 2-quart tube or bundt pan.

Cream butter and sugar well. Add eggs one at a time, beating well after each one. Add vanilla. Add flour 1 cup at a time, mixing in ⅓ of the buttermilk after each cup. Bake for 1 hour and 40 minutes.

Recipe taken from "Thirty Years at the Mansion" by Elizabeth Ashley.

DonnaAxum Whitworth

Born in El Dorado, Arkansas, Whitworth was Miss America in 1964.

"I've been in love with the beauty of Arkansas all my life, but northwest Arkansas' mountain ranges are my favorites. God's beauty abounds from the Wilhamena State Park at Mena to the beautiful Boston Mountain range between Alma and Fayetteville. And a float trip down the White River or a visit to picturesque Eureka Springs are also high on my list of beautiful memories."

Heavenly Rum Cake

1 package butter cake mix
1 package vanilla pudding
½ cup vegetable oil
½ cup light rum
4 eggs
½ cup water
½ cup chopped nuts

Glaze:
½ stick butter
½ cup sugar
½ cup water
½ cup rum

Preheat oven to 325°. Mix together in large bowl all cake ingredients using an electric mixer. Prepare a large bundt pan with baking spray (oil). Pour chopped nuts into bottom of pan. Pour the batter on top of the nuts. Bake for 50 to 60 minutes. Test for doneness with toothpick.

Allow cake to cool in bundt pan 10 minutes before removing. While cake is baking, mix the glazeingredients on the stove top slowly until thickened. Pour over warm cake.

Dinah Shore

Born in Winchester, Tennessee, Shore is a singer and actress who began singing in 1938. She has won 10 Emmys for various television shows.

Mother's Pecan Rum Cakes

Icing:
$\frac{1}{2}$ cup butter (1 stick)
$\frac{3}{4}$ pound powdered sugar, sifted
4 tablespoons milk
$1\frac{1}{2}$ teaspoons vanilla
salt
pecans, finely chopped

4 egg whites, warmed to room temperature
$2\frac{1}{4}$ cups sifted cake flour
$1\frac{1}{2}$ cups sugar
$3\frac{1}{2}$ teaspoons baking powder
$\frac{1}{2}$ cup softened butter, margarine or shortening
1 teaspoon salt
$\frac{3}{4}$ cup milk
$1\frac{1}{2}$ teaspoon vanilla
$\frac{1}{2}$ teaspoon rum extract
$\frac{1}{4}$ cup rum

Preheat oven to 350°. Sift flour, sugar, salt and baking powder into large bowl of mixer. Add shortening or butter, milk and vanilla; beat on slow speed until blended. Beat at medium speed for 2 minutes, occasionally scraping sides of bowl with rubber scraper. Add unbeaten egg whites, rum extract and rum; beat 2 minutes longer at medium speed.

Pour batter into one long 13 x 9 x $2\frac{1}{2}$-inch pan (or two 8-inch pans) that has been greased and floured and lined with wax paper. Bake for 35 to 40 minutes or until surface springs back when gently pressed with finger tips. While cake cools, prepare icing.

To prepare the icing, cream butter and sugar with hand beater until fluffy. Add salt and stir in milk, beating until very fluffy. Add vanilla and mix well.

When cake is completely cool, cut into $1\frac{1}{2}$-inch squares. Pour a generous teaspoon of rum on each cake square and then spread icing on all sides and roll in chopped fresh pecans.

The icing part is pretty messy, but it all comes out beautifully as you roll it around in the chopped nuts. I use a chopping bowl for this. You can substitute moist coconut for nuts and you have snow rum balls instead of pecan rum cakes. Or, if you leave out the rum, you have plain snow balls, which are great too. Make them $2\frac{1}{2}$ inches square and you have a dessert dish instead of an accompaniment.

Makes about 40 little cakes.

Recipe taken from: "Someone's in the Kitchen with Dinah," published by Doubleday and Company.

Erskine Caldwell

Born in White Oak, Georgia, Caldwell was an author known for earthy depictions of the rural poor: God's Little Acre, *1933, filmed 1958, and* Tobacco Road, *1932, filmed 1941. Caldwell died in 1987.*

"The Southern states hold a great fascination that is always changing and is never dull. I could never give preference to one over another anymore than I would with my four children."

Georgia Chip Bars

2⅓ cups sifted all-purpose flour
½ teaspoon baking powder
¼ teaspoon salt
1 cup margarine

1 cup brown sugar
1 teaspoon vanilla
1 package chocolate chips (12 ounces)
¾ cup chopped peanuts

Preheat oven to 350°. Sift flour, baking powder and salt. In separate bowl beat together butter, sugar and vanilla. Add dry ingredients and mix well. Stir in chopped nuts and chocolate chips.

Press dough firmly into well greased 15 x 10 x 1-inch baking pan. Bake for 20 to 25 minutes until lightly browned. While still hot, cut into bars of desired size.

Recipe should make 30 large or 60 small bars.

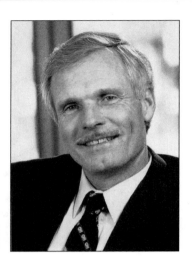

Ted Turner

Born in Cincinnati, Ohio, and living in Atlanta, Georgia, Turner is the colorful winner of the America's Cup in 1974 and 1977. He is also owner of the 1991 National League Champion Atlanta Braves baseball team and the Atlanta Hawks basketball team and founder of Atlanta-based Turner Broadcasting System and Cable News Network.

Haystack Cookies

12 ounces chocolate chip semi-sweet morsels
12 ounces butterscotch morsels
6 ounces chow mein noodles
1½ cups Planters dry roasted peanuts

In a heavy duty pot melt the chocolate chip semi-sweet and butterscotch morsels. Add the noodles and peanuts and mix all ingredients well. Drop on wax paper, refrigerate 5 minutes and serve.

Archie Manning

Born in Cleveland, Mississippi, Manning was a quarter-back in the National Football League in 1971-84, playing mostly for the New Orleans Saints. He led the NFL in pass completions in 1972.

"My favorite place to visit is Oxford, Mississippi. I'm sure I'm prejudiced because that's where I attended college, but it's a wonderful little town and the university is absolutely beautiful."

Lace Cookies

2 cups old-fashioned rolled oats
1 tablespoon flour
2 cups white sugar
2 sticks melted butter (1 cup)

2 eggs, beaten
1 teaspoon vanilla
$\frac{1}{2}$ teaspoon salt

Preheat oven to 325°. Put the oats, flour, sugar and salt into a large bowl and mix well. Pour very hot butter over the mixture and stir until the sugar is melted. Add the eggs and vanilla; stir well. Cover cookie sheets with aluminum foil (ungreased). Drop level $\frac{1}{2}$ teaspoon of mixture on foil, 2 inches apart. Cooking time is about 10 to 12 minutes. Watch carefully.

When cookies are completely cooled, foil will peel off. Store in airtight containers.

Makes about 6 dozen.

Jim "Catfish" Hunter

Born in Hertford, North Carolina, Hunter was a major league pitcher from 1965 to 1979. He threw a perfect game in 1968 and was inducted into the Baseball Hall of Fame in 1987.

"My family and I enjoy going to Nags Head, North Carolina, in the summer. We enjoy walking on the beach and just relaxing from our busy schedule."

Apple Pie

1 unbaked pie shell (9 inch)
5 cups sliced apples or 1 can Thank you brand
    sliced apples in water (20 ounces)
⅓ cup margarine, melted
¾ cup fructose

⅓ cup all-purpose flour
1 egg
1 teaspoon cinnamon
½ teaspoon nutmeg

Preheat oven to 350°. Place apples in pie shell. Combine remaining ingredients and pour over apples. Bake at 350° for 1 hour 10 minutes.

Pat Boone

*Born in Florida and raised near Nashville, Tennessee,
Boone is a singer noted for his clean-cut image and white
buck shoes. He starred in "April Love" in 1957.*

*"My favorite spot in the whole world is the old porch swing
at Mama and Daddy's on the outskirts of Nashville. It's
where I grew up, and so many of my happiest memories are
etched into the angles and corners and smells of home.
Daddy bought 10 acres and the house in 1940. It was
almost out in the country then, but it's downright residential
now. The old house is the same and the acre and a half
lawn my brother and I used to mow with a clattering hand
mower is still intact. The tour buses go by there, and Mama and Daddy wave at them from the yard,
and when I'm sitting on that swing, I do too. Not all the tourists realize it, but they're looking at
heaven on earth."*

Deep Dish Pie

Filling:
4½ cups fresh fruit, sliced
1 teaspoon vanilla
⅓ to ½ cup honey (depending on fruit's sweetness)
1 tablespoon plus 1 teaspoon lemon juice
thickening (flour, arrowroot or quickcook
   tapioca)
spice - depending on type of fruit:
   apples - 1 teaspoon cinnamon; peaches or
   apricots - ½ teaspoon nutmeg, mace or all-
   spice; prunes or plums - ½ teaspoon cloves.

Dough:
1 cup unbleached flour
1½ teaspoon baking powder
2 teaspoons honey
4 tablespoons butter or shortening
⅓ cup milk or cream

Combine filling ingredients in a saucepan and heat. Place in 8-inch, square greased pan.

Combine dough ingredients with fork and mix lightly. On floured board, knead for a minute or two.
Roll out to cover 8-inch square greased pan. Cover the fruit with dough. Dot with 3 tablespoons
butter.

Sprinkle top with cinnamon and bake at 450° for 20 to 30 minutes. Serve with fresh cream.

Jerry Falwell

Former leader and founder of the Moral Majority, born in Lynchburg, Virginia, Dr. Falwell is the founder of the "Old-Time Gospel Hour," a syndicated religious television program, and serves as chancellor of Liberty University in Lynchburg.

"I would have to say Lynchburg is my favorite destination. I was born and raised there and even though I do quite a bit of traveling, I always try to get home each evening."

Peanut Butter Pie

4 ounces cream cheese
$1\frac{1}{3}$ cup crunchy peanut butter
3 cups Cool Whip

$1\frac{1}{2}$ teaspoons honey, optional
1 cup powdered sugar
1 graham cracker pie crust

Mix cream cheese till fluffy, add sugar and beat until smooth. Add the peanut butter and honey and mix well. Fold in Cool Whip and pour into pie crust. Chill for 2 hours.

Joe Frank Harris

Born in Cartersville, Georgia, Harris is the former
governor of Georgia.

"My favorite destination is the north Georgia mountains,
equally as beautiful in the spring with the dogwood and
native plants blooming through the summer and fall, when
the color is at its peak. Golfing, fishing in the mountain
streams, hiking or skiing in the winter months provides a
variety of outdoor activity and sightseeing pleasure
throughout the year."

Peanut Butter Pie

1 chocolate crumb pie crust (10 inch)
1 quart vanilla ice cream, slightly softened
3/4 cup creamy peanut butter
1 cup unsalted peanuts, chopped

1 tablespoon vanilla
whipped cream, sweetened
hot fudge sauce

Combine ice cream, peanut butter, 1/2 cup peanuts and vanilla in bowl and mix well. Pour mixture into prepared crust and sprinkle with remaining nuts. Freeze overnight.

Remove from freezer about 10 minutes before serving, garnish with whipped cream and serve with hot fudge drizzled over each slice.

Strom Thurmond

Born in Edgefield, South Carolina, Thurmond — a conservative Democrat then Republican — has served as a United States senator from South Carolina since 1955. He is known for conducting the longest Senate filibuster, 24 hours, in 1957.

"My favorite travel destination for a vacation in the South is Kiawah Island, just off the coast of Charleston. I feel that Kiawah Island has a certain type of beauty and Southern charm that is unique. Of course, I am partial to the South as a whole."

South Carolina Pecan Pie

3 eggs
1 cup dark brown sugar
1 cup light corn syrup
1 tablespoon melted oleo

⅛ teaspoon salt
1 teaspoon vanilla extract
1 cup chopped pecans
9-inch pastry shell

Beat eggs, adding sugar gradually. Add syrup, oleo, vanilla and pecans. Pour into pastry shell. Bake at 360° for 1 hour.

Ronnie Milsap

Born in Robinsville, North Carolina, Milsap is a country music performer whose hit songs have included "Almost Like A Song," "Smoky Mountain Rain" and "Any Day Now."

"My favorite destination, naturally, is North Carolina. That's where I was born and raised, and just getting the opportunity to visit my home area at the foot of the Smokies always gives me an inner peace and perspective I don't seem to get anywhere else in the world. I made the statement in my autobiography that 'memories never die in the mountains,' and that's right ... they don't!"

Shortcake Pie

1 stick margarine
⅓ cup sugar
1 cup flour
2 eggs, separated

¼ teaspoon baking soda
1 teaspoon vanilla
4 tablespoons sugar
2 pints fresh strawberries, cleaned and sliced

Mix ⅓ cup sugar, 1 cup flour and soda together. Add margarine, egg yolks and vanilla. Pat crust in pie pan. Bake at 350° for 30 minutes. Fill with cleaned strawberries. Beat egg whites with remaining sugar and top pie. Brown meringue in oven. Chill and serve.

MaryAnnMobley

Born in Biloxi, Mississippi, Mobley is an actress and was crowned Miss America 1959. She was awarded a Golden Globe Award in 1965 as "The International Female Star of Tomorrow," and has appeared in numerous stage productions, films and television series including "Diff'rent Strokes," "Love Boat," "Hotel," and "Murder She Wrote."

"I love the South but I especially love my home state of Mississippi. I love it in so many ways; the flavors and sights of my home; the warmth and hospitality of its people; their sense of humor and their dignity and honor. It will always be my home, no matter where I may live."

PeachCobbler

6 to 8 large, very ripe fresh peaches peeled, seeded and sliced thin	1 cup self-rising flour
or	2 cups sugar
1 large can sliced, cling peaches	1 cup milk
1 stick butter	vanilla ice cream, optional

If using fresh peaches, peel and slice peaches and place in plastic bowl with 1 cup of sugar. Stir well and cover tightly. Refrigerate for 2 hours.

Place butter in bottom of rectangular pyrex baking dish (dish should be about 3 inches deep). Put in oven at 400° until butter melts. In a separate bowl, mix 1 cup self-rising flour, 1 cup sugar and 1 cup milk. Beat well with a whisk. Pour the mixture over melted butter (don't mix). Spoon peaches over batter mixture. If using canned peaches, add only a small amount of juice from can. If using fresh peaches, use natural juices. Bake at 400° until top becomes golden brown, about 1 hour.

Note: Very important — do not stir peaches into batter. The mixture rises up around the peaches and turns golden brown.

Serving Suggestion:
Serve hot with vanilla ice cream.

Brennan's Restaurant

World famous for its breakfast, Brennan's has been a New Orleans French Quarter landmark since 1946 and serves French Creole at its best. The restaurant, looking out on a lush, award-winning courtyard, gives diners the feeling of visiting a stately mansion. French doors grace windows overlooking a lace wrought-iron balcony which beckons visitors to enter through a picturesque carriageway.

Michael Roussel, Chef

"This is one of Brennan's most famous and most popular desserts. It's really quite simple to prepare. Wait until the rum gets hot, so that you get a good flame when it's ignited. This can also be prepared over a stove burner, then brought to the dinner table and flamed."

Bananas Foster

4 tablespoons butter
1 cup brown sugar
½ teaspoon cinnamon
4 tablespoons banana liqueur

4 bananas, cut in half lengthwise, then halved
¼ cup rum
4 scoops vanilla ice cream

Melt the butter over an alcohol burner in a flambé pan or attractive skillet. Add sugar, cinnamon, and banana liqueur and stir to mix. Heat for a few minutes, then place the bananas in the sauce and saute until soft and slightly browned.

Add the rum and allow it to heat well. Tip the pan so that the flame from the burner causes the sauce to light. Allow the sauce to flame until it dies out, tipping the pan with a circular motion to prolong the flaming. First lift the bananas carefully out of the pan and place four pieces over each portion of ice cream, then spoon the hot sauce from the pan over the top.

Sam Nunn

Born in Perry, Georgia, Nunn has served as a conservative Democratic senator for Georgia since 1972 and the chairman of the Senate Armed Forces Committee since 1987.

"Georgia is special to me because it is home, but for any traveler, Georgia provides a wide variety of special experiences: from the blue-misted 'hills of Habersham' that inspired poet Sidney Lanier, to the coastal islands, with their moss-hung live oaks and many unspoiled beaches which were once the exclusive preserves of millionaires. Spring and fall are my favorite times to get away to a mountain cabin and spend time with my family in the woods as the seasons change. My daughter and I spent a unique vacation while she was home from college. We explored the Okefenokee Swamp, the remote, mysterious 'land of the trembling earth,' which is the source of both the Suwannee River and Walt Kelly's Pogo."

Double Chocolate Brownies

¾ cups all-purpose flour
¼ teaspoon baking soda
¼ teaspoon salt
⅓ cup butter
2 tablespoons water
¾ cup sugar

1 package semi-sweet chocolate chips (12 ounces)
1 teaspoon vanilla
2 eggs
½ cup chopped pecans

In small bowl combine flour, baking soda and salt, set aside. In small saucepan combine butter, sugar and water, bring just to a boil and remove from heat. Add 6 ounces of the chocolate chips and vanilla; stir until melted and mixture is smooth. Transfer to a large bowl. Add eggs, one at a time, beating after each addition. Gradually blend in flour mixture and stir in chopped nuts and chocolate chips. Pour into greased 9-inch square baking pan and bake at 325° for 40 to 45 minutes.

Letitia Baldrige

Born in Miami Beach, Florida, Baldrige is a public relations executive and served as social secretary at the White House during the Kennedy administration, 1961-63.

"My car broke down near Louisville. As a cynical New Yorker, I could not believe that the first person I signalled in a passing truck hauled me into town to a garage and the garage owner fed me half of his delicious lunch. If this same episode had occurred near New York, I'd still be on the road trying to flag someone down to help!

"Two places I most love to visit in the South are Atlanta, Georgia, and Linville, North Carolina. I visit Atlanta every month on business and I find the restaurants are better than any place in America. For tranquility, I go to Eeseloa Lodge in the Blue Ridge Mountains of Linville, North Carolina. It is one of the most beautiful places I have been. I go there to write, play croquet and laugh at all the people playing golf."

La Meilleure Creme Brulee

2 cups heavy cream
½ cup plus 3 tablespoons dark brown sugar

¼ cup plus 3 tablespoons brandy
4 egg yolks, slightly beaten

Preheat oven to 250°. Heat cream in top of double boiler over medium high heat; do not boil. Remove from heat and stir in 3 tablespoons brown sugar and 3 tablespoons brandy. Slowly whisk hot cream into egg yolks and pour mixture into an 8-inch glass shallow baking dish.

Place the filled baking dish into a larger pan and carefully add enough hot water to come halfway up the baking dish. Bake for 1½ hours, or until custard is set and knife inserted near center comes out clean. Carefully remove baking dish from water. Let cool, uncovered, to room temperature. Cover and refrigerate 8 hours or overnight.

About 2 hours before serving, have broiler well preheated. Sift remaining ½ cup sugar over custard, making an even topping. Watching carefully so that the sugar does not burn, broil 8 inches from heat source for 1 to 3 minutes, until sugar is evenly browned and crusted. Cover the custard and refrigerate until thoroughly chilled.

Before serving, pour ¼ cup brandy over the custard to soften the crust and enhance flavor.

Crescent Dragonwagon

Born in New York City but moved to Eureka Springs, Arkansas, in 1971, Dragonwagon is an author of almost 20 books, including one novel, one young adult novel, three cookbooks and a book of poetry.

"When I happened onto the Victorian Ozark Mountain resort town of Eureka Springs, Arkansas, I was so captivated I moved here at once. Not only have I lived here since, but when I married, my husband and I told our friends that we'd be honeymooning in Galveston ... when, in reality, we left on the highway only to sneak back to Eureka on a back road, managing three lovely and undetected days in the town we love best. We now run an inn, Dairy Hollow House, and have the pleasure of watching visitors melt into the place much as we did, and do."

Dairy Hollow House Gingerbread

1½ cups unbleached flour
1 cup sugar
2 teaspoons ginger
1 teaspoon cinnamon
½ cup shortening
1 egg

3 tablespoons blackstrap molasses
1 cup buttermilk
1 teaspoon baking soda
1 scant teaspoon salt

Preheat oven to 350°.

Combine flour, sugar and spices. Cut in shortening until crumbly, and reserve ¼ cup of the mixture. Dissolve salt and baking soda in the buttermilk. Add buttermilk, molasses and egg to the flour mixture and mix well. Pour into a well-greased 8- or 9-inch skillet and sprinkle with reserved mix and bake 30 minutes.

Serving Suggestion:
Serve with whipped cream, ice cream or a baked apple.

Pat Head Summitt

Born in Clarksville, Tennessee, Summitt is the head basketball coach of the University of Tennessee Lady Volunteers. As a player, she won an Olympic Silver Medal in 1976, and as a coach she brought home the first USA Gold Medal in Olympic competition in 1984. She led her Tennessee teams to NCAA National Championships in 1987, 1989 and 1991.

"San Destin, Florida. I love the white sand, blue water, great eating places and it is not overcrowded."

Homemade Ice Cream

3½ cups sugar
5 eggs
1 heaping tablespoon flour
1 pint whipping cream

dash salt
2 tablespoons vanilla extract
3 quarts plus ½ cup milk

Beat whole eggs and add ½ cup milk. Gradually add the flour and sugar and remaining milk. Beat well. Cook at low temperature until coats spoon. Remove from heat and cool. Add the whipping cream, salt and vanilla. Freeze.

May cut down 2 cups of milk and add fruit if desired.

Dolly Parton

Born in Sevier County, Tennessee, Parton is a country music entertainer and actress. Her hit records include "Here You Come Again," "Silver and Gold," "Two Doors Down," and "Eagle When She Flies." She has also starred in several movies including Nine to Five, Best Little Whore House in Texas, *and* Steel Magnolias.

"Tennessee is always my favorite destination because it is now and always will be home ... and, you know, there's no place like home!"

Islands in the Stream

3 eggs, separated
⅔ cup sugar
2 heaping teaspoons flour

1 quart milk
1 teaspoon vanilla
nutmeg, optional

Cream egg yolks with sugar and whip until smooth, add flour and mix well. Scald the milk, and when hot enough, add the cream mixture. Stir constantly 20 to 25 minutes until it thickens, remove from heat and add vanilla.

Boil some water. Whip egg whites and add to water until hardened. Remove with spatula and put on top of the cream mixture. Sprinkle with nutmeg. Chill.

— B —

Bacon
Stuffed Bacon Rolls ....Teddy Gentry 9
Bacon and Cheese Bread ....Wayne Newton 27

Beef
Anytime Briskett of Beef ....Steve Lundquist 39
Burt's Beef Stew ....Burt Reynolds 44
Charcoaled Roast...............................Bert Lance 42
Chris's Spaghetti ....Chris Evert 45
Corned Beef Casserole ....George Hamilton IV 46
Grillades ....William J. Guste, Jr. 41
Hamburger - Vegetable Chowder ....Naomi Judd 22
Horkies (pigs in a blanket) ....Don Garlits 52
Hungarian Goulash............................Ned Beatty 49
Perk Up Soup ....Jerry Lee Lewis 23
Raymone's Beenie Weenies ....Ray Stevens 51
Salt Steak...Walker Percy 43
Sloppy Joe's ....Stan Smith 47
Stuffed Green Peppers.......................Richard Petty 48
Tartare Good Old Boy ....Jack Butler 13
Viennese Goulash ....Rosemary Clooney 50

Black-eyed peas
Hoppin' John ....Mitch McConnell 99

Breads
Bacon and Cheese Bread ....Wayne Newton 27
Dairy Hollow House Gingerbread.......Crescent Dragonwagon 134
Lucy Ford's Biscuits ....Kenneth Noland 28
Popovers ....J. William Fulbright 33
Georgia Peach Bread ....Sam Nunn 35
Kay's Blueberry Muffins ....Bob Timberlake 34

Brownies
Double Chocolate Brownies................Sam Nunn 132

— C —

Cabbage
Smothered Cabbage............................Carroll Angelle 93

Cakes

Angel Food Cake	Richard Petty	111
Cocoa Raspberry Cake	Frank Hickingbotham	113
Coconut Cake	Naomi Judd	114
Fresh Apple Cake	Guy Hunt	112
German Chocolate Double Delight	B. B. King	116
Little Wonder Chocolate Cake	Holly Hunter	117
Pound Cake	Bill Clinton	118
Heavenly Rum Cake	Donna Axum Whitworth	119
Mother's Pecan Rum Cakes	Dinah Shore	120

Cheese

Cottage Cheese Salad	Vanna White	18
Pimento Cheese Spread	Bart Starr	10
Sweet Brie	Vince Dooley	12

Chicken

Chicken and Wild Rice Casserole	Elizabeth Dole	53
Chicken Breast Casserole	Ronnie Milsap	56
Chicken, Broccoli and Rice Casserole	Brooks Robinson	62
Chicken Enchiladas	Bill Clinton	57
Chicken Melanzana with Spaghetti	Terry Bradshaw	58
Chicken Spectacular	Davey Allison	59
Chinese Chicken with Walnuts	Al Gore, Jr.	63
Chunky Chicken Salad	Claude Pepper	17
Corn and Chicken Casserole	Paul Prudhomme	64
Hawaiian Barbecue Chicken	Steve Garvey	66
Lemon Chicken Scallopini	Tommy Newsom	67
My Mother's Chicken Spaghetti	Craig Claiborne	60
Roast Boneless Chicken Legs	Don Tyson	54
Ruth Malone's Chicken Pie	Ruth Malone	68
Sweetness Chicken	Walter Payton	69

Cookies

Georgia Chip Bars	Erskine Caldwell	121
Haystack Cookies	Ted Turner	122
Lace Cookies	Archie Manning	123

Corn

Corn Pudding	Alex Haley	94

Cornbread and Dressing

Cornbread Dressing ....Jim Nabors 32
Lucy Ford's Cornbread ....Kenneth Noland 28
Old-Fashioned Cornbread Dressing ....Tennessee Ernie Ford 31
Pea-Picker's Cornbread ....Tennessee Ernie Ford 31
Spicy Hot Cornbread ....Beth Henley 29

Crab

Crab Cakes ....Sea Captain's House 75
Norfolk Crab Cakes ....John Warner 76

Cucumbers

Cucumber Dip ....Bart Starr 10

Custards

Islands in the Stream ....Dolly Parton 136
La Meilleure Creme Brulee ....Letitia Baldrige 133

— E —

Eggs

Eggs Somerset ....John Sherman Cooper 88
Gin Fizz Egg Pie ....Theodore Taylor 89
Seafarer's Omelette ....Sea Captain's House 87

— F —

Fish

Grouper Bienville ....Cafe Creole 80
President Carter's Fried Fish Recipe ....Jimmy Carter 79
Trout Stuffed with Cedar Berries ....Billy Joe Tatum 82

Fruit

Bananas Foster ....Brennan's Restaurant 131
Fresh Fruit with Orange-Pecan Dressing ......Jim Varney 19
Georgia Peach Bread ....Sam Nunn 35
Kay's Blueberry Muffins ....Bob Timberlake 34

— G —

Game

Anabaptist Rabbit ....Will D. Campbell 70
Venison or Elk Stew ....Joe B. Hall 73

Grits

Cheese Grits Souffle .... Marsha Norman 96
Cheese Grits Souffle .... Willard Scott 97
Grits with Cream .... Nathalie Dupree 98
Guste Grits .... William J. Guste, Jr. 40

— H —

Ices and Ice Cream

Homemade Ice Cream .... Pat Head Summitt 135
Orange Ice .... Naomi Judd 114

— L —

Lamb

Barbecued Butterflied Leg of Lamb .... Donald Harrington 71
Sailboat Chili .... James Martin 72

— M —

Macaroni and Cheese

Famous Macaroni and Cheese .... Rufus Thomas 101
Macaroni and Cheese .... Minnie Pearl 102

— O —

Onions

Onion Pie .... Eudora Welty 103

Oysters

Oysters Bienville .... Ray Mabus 11

— P —

Pies

Apple Pie .... Jim "Catfish" Hunter 124
Deep Dish Pie .... Pat Boone 125
Peach Cobbler .... Mary Ann Mobley 130
Peanut Butter Pie .... Jerry Falwell 126
Peanut Butter Pie .... Joe Frank Harris 127
Shortcake Pie .... Ronnie Millsap 129
South Carolina Pecan Pie .... Strom Thurmond 128

Potatoes

Cheesy New Potatoes ....Minnie Pearl 102
Potato Casserole ....The Statler Brothers 104
Georgia Sweet Potato Souffle ....Joe Frank Harris 106
Sweet Potato Casserole ....Randy Travis 107

— R —

Rice

Lucille's Dirty Rice ....Geoffrey Beene 100

— S —

Salad Dressing

Fresh Fruit with Orange-Pecan Dressing ......Jim Varney 19
Mary Alice's Salad Dressing.......................Albert B. "Happy" Chandler 20

Seafood

Crescent City Soup ....Ellis Marsalis 21
Seafarer's Omelette ....Sea Captain's House 87
Seafood Gumbo ....John Folse 74

Shrimp

Cajun Shrimp ....Deborah Norville 83
Crawfish and Noodles ....Buddy Roemer 78
Low Country Shrimp and Sausage ....Carroll A. Campbell 84
Shrimp Etouffee ....Carroll Angelle 85
Shrimp in Wine Sauce, Low Country Style ..John Jakes..86

Squash

Henry Davis' Baked Cushaw ....Ellen Douglas 95
Stir-Fry American Style ....Ronnie Milsap 105

Sweet Potatoes

Georgia Sweet Potato Souffle ....Joe Frank Harris 106
Sweet Potato Casserole ....Randy Travis 107

— A —

Allison, Davey .... Chicken Spectacular 59
Angelle, Carroll .... Shrimp Etouffee 85
                                             Smothered Cabbage 93
Axum Whitworth, Donna .... Heavenly Rum Cake 119

— B —

Baldrige, Letitia .... La Meilleure Creme Brulee 133
Beatty, Ned .... Hungarian Goulash 49
Beene, Geoffrey .... Lucille's Dirty Rice 100
Boone, Pat .... Deep Dish Pie 125
Bradshaw, Terry .... Chicken Melanzana with Spaghetti 58
Brennan's Restaurant .... Bananas Foster 131
Butler, Jack .... Tartare Good Old Boy 13

— C —

Cafe Creole .... Grouper Bienville 80-81
Caldwell, Erskine .... Georgia Chip Bars 121
Campbell, Carroll A., Jr. .... Low Country Shrimp and Sausage 84
Campbell, Will D. .... Anabaptist Rabbit 70
Carter, Jimmy .... President Carter's Fried Fish Recipe 79
Chandler, Albert B. "Happy" .... Mary Alice's Salad Dressing 20
Claiborne, Craig .... My Mother's Chicken Spaghetti 60-61
Clinton, Bill .... Chicken Enchiladas 57
                                             Pound Cake 118
Clooney, Rosemary .... Viennese Goulash 50
Cooper, John Sherman .... Eggs Somerset 88

— D —

Dole, Elizabeth .... Chicken and Wild Rice Casserole 53
Dooley, Vince .... Sweet Brie 12
Douglass, Ellen .... Henry Davis' Baked Cushaw 95
Dragonwagon, Crescent .... Dairy Hollow House Gingerbread 134
Dupree, Nathalie .... Grits with Cream 98

— E —

Evert, Chris .... Chris's Spaghetti 45

— F —

Falwell, Jerry .... Peanut Butter Pie 126
Folse, John .... Louisiana Seafood Gumbo 74
Ford, Tennessee Ernie .... Pea-Picker's Cornbread 30-31
Old-Fashioned Cornbread Dressing 30-31
Fulbright, Honorable J. William .... Popovers 33

— G —

Garlits, Don .... Horkies (pigs in a blanket) 52
Garvey, Steve .... Hawaiian Barbecue Chicken 66
Gentry, Teddy .... Stuffed Bacon Rolls 9
Gore, Al, Jr. .... Chinese Chicken with Walnuts 63
Guste, William J., Jr. .... Guste Grits and Grillades 40-41

— H —

Haley, Alex .... Corn Pudding 94
Hall, Joe B. .... Venison or Elk Stew 73
Hamilton, George, IV .... Corned Beef Casserole 46
Harrington, Donald .... Barbecued Butterflied Leg of Lamb 71
Harris, Joe Frank .... Georgia Sweet Potato Souffle 106
Peanut Butter Pie 127
Henley, Beth .... Spicy Hot Cornbread 29
Hickingbotham, Frank .... Cocoa Raspberry Cake 113
Hunt, Guy .... Fresh Apple Cake 112
Hunter, Holly .... Little Wonder Chocolate Cake 117
Hunter, Jim "Catfish" .... Apple Pie 124

— J —

Jakes, John .... Shrimp in Wine Sauce, Low Country Style 86
Judd, Naomi .... Coconut Cake 114
Hamburger-Vegetable Chowder 22
Orange Ice 114

— K —

King, B. B. .... B.B.'s German Chocolate Double Delight 116

— L —

Lance, Bert .... Charcoaled Roast 42
Lewis, Jerry Lee .... Perk Up Soup 23
Lundquist, Steve .... Anytime Briskett of Beef 39

— M —

Mabus, Ray .... Oysters Bienville 11
Malone, Ruth .... Ruth Malone's Chicken Pie 68
Manning, Archie .... Lace Cookies 123
Marsalis, Ellis .... Crescent City Soup 21
Martin, James .... Sailboat Chili 72
McConnell, Mitch .... Hoppin' John 99
Milsap, Ronnie .... Chicken Breast Casserole 56
                                            Shortcake Pie 129
                                            Stir-Fry American Style 105
Mobley, Mary Ann .... Peach Cobbler 130

— N —

Nabors, Jim .... Cornbread Dressing 32
Newsom, Tommy .... Lemon Chicken Scallopini 67
Newton, Wayne .... Bacon and Cheese Bread 27
Noland, Kenneth .... Lucy Ford's Cornbread 28
                                            Lucy Ford's Biscuits 28
Norman, Marsha .... Cheese Grits Souffle 96
Norville, Deborah .... Cajun Shrimp 83
Nunn, Sam .... Double Chocolate Brownies 132
                                            Georgia Peach Bread 35

— P —

Parton, Dolly .... Islands in the Stream 136
Payton, Walter .... Sweetness Chicken 69
Pearl, Minnie .... Cheesy New Potatoes 102
                                            Macaroni and Cheese 102
Pepper, Claude .... Chunky Chicken Salad 17
Percy, Walker .... Salt Steak 43
Petty, Richard .... Angel Food Cake 111
                                            Stuffed Bell Peppers 48
Prudhomme, Paul .... Corn and Chicken Casserole 64-65

— R —

Reynolds, Burt .... Burt's Beef Stew 44
Robinson, Brooks .... Chicken, Broccoli and Rice Casserole 62
Roemer, Buddy .... Crawfish and Noodles 78

— S —

Scott, Willard .... Cheese Grits Souffle 97
Sea Captain's House .... Crab Cakes 75
                                        Seafarer's Omelette 87
Shore, Dinah .... Mother's Pecan Rum Cakes 120
Smith, Stan .... Sloppy Joe's 47
Starr, Bart .... Cucumber Dip 10
                                        Pimento Cheese Spread 10
                                        Coconut Pecan Cake 115
Statler Brothers, The .... Potato Casserole 104
Stevens, Ray .... Raymone's Beanie Weenies 51
Summitt, Pat Head .... Homemade Ice Cream 135

— T —

Tatum, Billy Joe .... Trout Stuffed with Cedar Berries 82
Taylor, Theodore .... Gin Fizz Egg Pie 89
Thomas, Rufus .... Famous Macaroni and Cheese 101
Thurmond, Strom .... South Carolina Pecan Pie 128
Timberlake, Bob .... Kay's Blueberry Muffins 34
Travis, Randy .... Sweet Potato Casserole 107
Turner, Ted .... Haystack Cookies 122
Tyson, Don .... Roast Boneless Chicken Legs 54-55

— V —

Varney, Jim .... Fresh Fruit with Orange-Pecan Dressing 19

— W —

Warner, John .... Norfolk Crab Cakes 76-77
Welty, Eudora .... Onion Pie 103
White, Vanna .... Cottage Cheese Salad 18